They were all impressed with your Halston dress
And the people that you knew at Elaine's

—BILLY JOEL, "BIG SHOT"

EVERYONE COMES TO

EVERYONE COMES TO

FORTY YEARS OF
MOVIE STARS,
ALL-STARS,
LITERARY LIONS,
FINANCIAL SCIONS,
TOP COPS,
POLITICIANS,
AND POWER BROKERS
AT THE LEGENDARY HOT SPOT

A. E. HOTCHNER

HarperEntertainment
An Imprint of HarperCollins*Publishers*

Permission to excerpt Gael Greene's articles about Elaine's is generously granted by Ms. Greene.

Permission to use Bruce Jay Friedman's reflections generously granted by Mr. Friedman.

All photograph credits appear on page 233.

Unless otherwise indicated, all photographs and drawings are from the personal collection of Elaine Kaufman.

HarperCollins books may be purchased for educational, business, or sales promotional use. For information please write: Special Markets Department, HarperCollins Publishers Inc., 10 East 53rd Street, New York, NY 10022.

FIRST EDITION

Designed by Walter Bernard
with Julia Zichello and Joe Maher

Printed on acid-free paper

Library of Congress Cataloging-in-Publication Data

    Hotchner, A. E.
       Everyone comes to Elaine's: forty years of movie stars, all-stars,
       literary lions, financial scions, top cops, politicians, and power
       brokers at the legendary hot spot / by A. E. Hotchner.—1st ed.
          p. cm.
       ISBN 0-06-053818-X
    1. Elaine's Restaurant (New York, N.Y.) 2. Kaufman, Elaine. I. Title

      TX945.5.E43H68   2004
      641.5'09747'1—dc22   2003056872

04 05 06 07 08 ❖/RRD 10 9 8 7 6 5 4 3 2 1

Here's to Virginia, Tracy, Holly, Timothy, Franklin,
and the years of good times we've had at Elaine's

ACKNOWLEDGMENTS

Preparing this book was a collective labor of love by the many people who are devoted to Elaine, but special recognition goes to Diane Becker, Bruce Jay Friedman, Winston Groom, Claire Panke, Gay Talese, Renee St. Jean, Kerry Goldstein, David Black, Nora Ephron, Jonathan Becker, Pete Hamill, Ron Galella, Owen Laster, and above all, Maureen O'Brien, as cheerful, precise, and knowledgeable an editor as a writer could hope for.

Much appreciation to my lovely Virginia Kiser who prodded, nudged, and nagged me to write this book, much like (figuratively) Mrs. Ruskin used her cat-o'-nine tails on John.

And thank you, Elaine, for your splendid cooperation along the way, the many interviews you endured with patience and good humor, and, particularly, your incisive observations on the human condition.

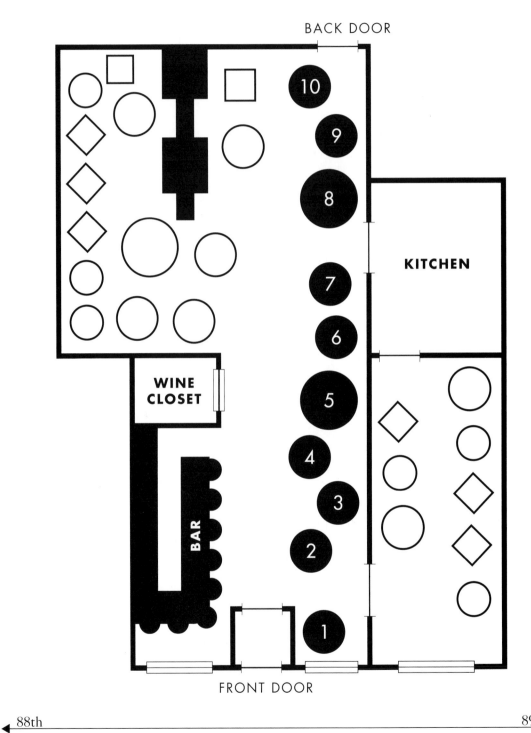

BACK DOOR

10

9

8

KITCHEN

7

6

5

WINE
CLOSET

4

3

BAR

2

1

FRONT DOOR

88th

89th

Second Avenue

THE TABLES AT ELAINE'S

1

Mary Higgins Clark, Susan Sontag, Lauren Bacall, Helen Frankenthaler, Frederic Morton, Liz Smith, Mayor David Dinkins, Father Pete Colapietro

2

Walt Frazier, Keith Hernandez, Mark Messier, Derek Jeter, Pete Hamill, Arnold Schwarzenegger, Patrick Ewing, Rudolf Nureyev

3

Larry L. King, Joe DiMaggio, Joe Namath, Wayne Gretzky, Sylvester Stallone, Dan Jenkins, Noel Coward, Laurence Olivier

4

Norman Mailer, Gay Talese, Winston Groom, William Styron, Tom Wolfe, A. E. Hotchner, Bruce Jay Friedman, Irwin Shaw, Jack Richardson, Arthur Kopit, Kurt Vonnegut, James Jones, David Halberstam

5

Marlon Brando, Tony Bennett, Mike Wallace, Geraldo Rivera, Jerry Orbach, Albert Finney, Cy Coleman, Robert Altman, Calvin Klein

6

Frank Sinatra, Molly Ringwald, Arthur Miller, Sharon Stone, Yo-Yo Ma, Nora Ephron, Nick Pileggi, Sydney Pollack

7

Michael Caine, Mikhail Baryshnikov, Liza Minnelli, Judy Garland, Barbra Streisand, Al Pacino, Michelle Pfeiffer, Mick Jagger

8

Woody Allen, Robin Williams, George Steinbrenner, George Plimpton, Hillary Clinton, Bobby Short, Jessye Norman, Dominick Dunne

9

Andy Warhol, Tennessee Williams, Dustin Hoffman, Martha Stewart, George Balanchine, Isaac Stern, Clint Eastwood

10

Jackie Kennedy, Leonard Bernstein, Mike Nichols, Jimmy Carter, Jack Nicholson, Sean Connery, Elizabeth Taylor

There is no private house, in which people can enjoy themselves so well, as at a capital tavern. Let there be ever so great plenty of good things, ever so much grandeur, ever so much elegance, ever so much desire that everybody should be easy; in the nature of things it cannot be: there must always be some degree of care and anxiety. The master of the house is anxious to entertain his guests; the guests are anxious to be agreeable to him; and no man, but a very impudent dog indeed, can as freely command what is in another man's house, as if it were his own. Whereas, at a tavern, there is a general freedom from anxiety. You are sure you are welcome; and the more noise you make the more trouble you give, the more things you call for, the welcomer you are. No servants will attend you with the alacrity which waiters do, who are incited by the prospect of an immediate reward in proportion as they please. No, Sir; there is nothing which has yet been contrived by man, by which so much happiness is produced as by a good tavern or inn.

—SAMUEL JOHNSON

I first came to Elaine's about a year after it
opened, in the early sixties. I was broke at the time, laying low, trying
to organize a book about the years I knew Hemingway, but my friend,
Gay Talese, who had recently quit his reportorial job at the *New York
Times*, induced me to go with him to a place called Elaine's for a plate
of inexpensive spaghetti (it was, back then). I didn't know much about
the place other than, according to Gay, it was a writers' hangout run by
a hearty woman who read books.

It was a long way uptown, as the taxi meter testified, but going up
to that unexplored Yorktown area with its German trappings,
rathskellers, kaffeehäuser, Schaller und Weber, Janssens's, die kleine
konditorei, made it feel like an adventure.

And now, almost forty years later, it remains an adventure every
time I go through the double doors and enter the preserve that is
called a saloon by virtually everyone but Elaine, who despises the
word. In her mind, perhaps it conjures up the sawdust-on-the-floor,
swinging-door, gin mills of the Old West. Actually, according to the
unabridged *Century* dictionary, saloon and salon are interchangeable.
In fact, Elaine presides over her saloon/salon quite like Gertrude
Stein, also a lady of ample girth, presided over her salon in Paris in the
twenties. The Stein salon attracted young, promising writers and
artists—James Joyce, Sherwood Anderson, Hemingway, Dos Passos,
Picasso, Matisse—and Elaine has been mother hen to David Halberstam, Tom Wolfe, Gay Talese, William Styron, Pete Hamill, Norman
Mailer, Arthur Kopit, and scores of other young, unrecognized talents.
Gertrude Stein served plum wine and cookies, Elaine served calamari
and Chianti. Both ladies share a remarkable sensory ability for recog-
nizing unusual talent in its embryonic stage, and for being able to nur-

ture and promote it. It's unfortunate that the doyenne of rue de Fleurus and the patroness of Second Avenue never had the chance to meet and probe their remarkable affinity for talent.

Over the past couple of years, Elaine and I have had many talks about her personal life and the remarkable life she has created in her Manhattan citadel. These revelations plus contributions from a rainbow of writers and world figures who frequent her establishment grace many of these pages.

Getting back to the sense of adventure I feel on entering Elaine's, it's the tantalizing spirit of the place, the ebb and flow of arrivers and departers, table-hoppers who plunk themselves down for a couple of minutes, the milling, amorphous bar people who lead a life of their own, the camaraderie of waiters who sometimes philosophize while discussing the menu, but more than anything it's Elaine herself, stopping by to deliver spicy bulletins, greeting and kissing her friends, scolding waiters, seating her regulars at tables that mystically appear where there is no space for a table, pulling up a chair and joining a table, drinking coffee and enjoying the repartee of her favorites, enlarging a table for four to a table for ten faster than David Copperfield can conjure up an elephant, Elaine being the source of the warm, gemütlichkeit that fills the room and attracts remarkable people from all over the world. In a sense, Elaine's is a microcosm of the people and events of the last forty years, from the sixties, when Beatles and Stones held forth there, to the start of this century, when there were painful wakes for the Elaine's "regulars" who perished on September 11.

So, Elaine, you are both the last of the great saloon keepers and the hostess of a remarkable salon—take your pick.

// In a blood sense, I don't have a family, but what are you going to do if you're in a family? Hope you have someone there to talk to? I have it here. There are really terrific people to talk to every night. And that's the kind of family for me, I prefer my Elaine's family to a regular family because a family is always loaded with problems, which, as far as I am concerned, is really boring. But there has never been a night here when I've been bored. Not with the people who come to Elaine's. **//**

—ELAINE

Everyone Comes to Elaine's

1

Elaine's hosts many book parties
and events like this Academy Award
bash given by *Entertainment Weekly*

PHOTOGRAPH BY JESSICA BURSTEIN

What Rick's place was to Casablanca, Elaine's is to New York, the same swirling intrigue, international celebrities, double-dealing, jealousies, threats and brutalities, sentimentality, romance, sex and redemption, the only difference being that Humphrey Bogart played Rick on a Warner Bros. soundstage, whereas Elaine Kaufman plays her own improbable self at Eighty-eighth Street and Second Avenue in Manhattan. Elaine, a Jewish lady from the Bronx, who, for the past forty years, has presided over her exotic establishment, a mecca for the famous, the near famous, and the infamous.

Elaine's is where Mia Farrow asked Michael Caine to introduce her to Woody Allen; where the entire Rangers hockey team came at 3 A.M. after winning the Stanley Cup from which they drank an imposing quantity of beer; where Norman Mailer and the rock composer Jerry Leiber got into a roiling wrestling match that wound up tearing a hole in the side wall; where Reggie Jackson came the night he hit those historic home runs in the World Series; where Jackie Kennedy came the first night after her mourning period ended; where Frank Sinatra, on being introduced to Mario Puzo, author of *The Godfather*, refused to shake his hand.

Physically, the place is nothing much, but, as Nora Ephron says, "It has the greatest look of any New York saloon. The dark wood, the framed book jackets on the walls, the Bentwood chairs, the checkered tablecloths—it is just a physically perfect place." But beyond that, it also has an aura about it, a mysticism of exclusiveness, that makes it rather forbidding. On any given night, you cannot anticipate the mood within: serene (infrequently), blustery, combative, riotously festive, even, on occasion, rebellious. But whatever

On any given night, you cannot anticipate the mood within: serene (infrequently), blustery, combative, riotously festive, even, on occasion, rebellious.

the prevailing atmosphere, you can be sure that Elaine, like Rick, will be seated at one of the tables, monitoring the activities, the arrivals and departures, barmen and waiters occasionally whispering in her ear, favored guests being greeted and seated, offending patrons being castigated and occasionally excommunicated, in a nightly scene more suited to the stage of a Broadway theater than the rather seedy environs in which it is located.

Elaine with the cast of NBC's *Saturday Night Live*, circa 1970

Elaine's place has a distinguished ancestry. Beginning with flamboyant Texas Guinan in the Roaring Twenties, New York's nightlife has been steadily illuminated by a gaudy group of big-time saloon keepers, including Toots Shor, who began as a speakeasy bouncer; Jack Kreindler, who originally operated "21" as a speakeasy; the consummate Irishman Tim Costello, who started a speakeasy upstairs at Lexington and Forty-fourth with his brother, Joe; Dan Lavezzo of PJ Clarke's; Sherman Billingsley, a bootlegger from Oklahoma who started the Stork Club with two vicious gangsters, Dutch Schultz and Owney Madden, as his partners; Vincent Sardi; Joe Allen in his original place in the theater district. Each of these barons had a distinct fiefdom: Toots, a gargantuan, garrulous two-fisted drinker, catered to jocks, especially the New York Yankees; Kreindler's preserve embraced blue bloods, captains of industry, and politicians; Billingsley kowtowed to café society and Hollywood stars; Costello's was a watering hole for the prestigious writers and cartoonists of *The New Yorker;* Lavezzo, who was popular with musicians and singers, had a particular passion for the New York Giants football team, which he feted en masse; Sardi attracted Broadway headliners whereas Joe Allen was home to lesser Broadway performers who couldn't afford Sardi's, mostly chorus kids.

But these big-time saloons have diminished or disappeared from the New York scene: the establishments of Shor, Costello, Billingsley, and Lavezzo have passed on with their proprietors; Sardi's, "21," and Joe Allen have lost their originality, but Elaine, now in her fortieth year, thrives as a late-night phenomenon with no alternate place in sight—she may well be the last of the great saloon keepers.

At Elaine's, the food, décor, prices, service, and seating have all been subject to critical carping, yet on any given night, the clientele, ranging from Nobel Prize winners to rock stars, will outglitter that of any other establishment in the city, in fact, the world. Still, there are a large number of people, well known, rich, prestigious, who find the prospect of presenting themselves at Elaine's intimidating, who feel they need some kind of special entrée, afraid to enter if not accompanied by an accepted regular. The public perception of Elaine's—to an extent justified—is that of a forbidding, cliquish preserve restricted to the favorites of the lady whose name it bears, and outsiders wonder what qualifies those who dine at the favored tables. The irony is that few of the illustrious who do frequent Elaine's hallowed walls can explain why they are there.

It may well be that whereas her antecedents, from Texas Guinan's to Costello's to "21," were all speakeasies where the proprietors identified those they admitted after viewing them through a peephole, Elaine's is just as selective but with a figurative peephole.

How the favored occupants got there in the first place has to do with the fact that the early settlers around Elaine's checkered tablecloths were writers. Writers are pilot fish—they are fearless and adventure-prone and will go into any new, dark, uninviting place if it looks cheap, different, and indulgent about how long a table can be occupied. Writers like to sit at tables for a long time and not spend much money, or spend a great deal if they can put it on their tab. Either way, they are not a bonanza for a new restaurant.

When Elaine Kaufman, who helped run a restaurant called Portofino, at Thompson and Bleecker Streets in the Village, took her life savings in April 1963 and bought a rather drab Austro-Hungarian bar at Eighty-eighth and Second, some pilot fish writers

Writers like to sit at tables for a long time and not spend much money, or spend a great deal if they can put it on their tab.

came poking around. The editor and writer Nelson Aldrich lived around the corner, George Plimpton came in, the playwright Jack Richardson, Mary Ann Madden (she even painted the ladies' room for opening night), and word flashed through the scriveners' underground that Elaine's was choice waters. She not only let them linger at their tables and run up tabs but was amusing and sympathetic, and *she liked writers*.

Look, this is a late-night saloon and occasionally it's necessary to assert myself when things get a little out of hand.

"When I first stepped into Elaine's, in 1964, it was simply one large, permissive room," Jack Richardson says. "Second Avenue in the upper Eighties was then a fairly rough neighborhood, and it must be confessed that Elaine's reflected the area. Hookers squalled at the bar and arm wrestled for boilermakers; the jukebox boomed out polkas and German marches, music left over from the days the place had been a meeting spot for Yorkville Bundists; Irish workers from the local brewery battered one another into oblivion, puked, sang, and passed out with that lyrical charm for which their race is famous; and Madam herself waited on tables, gingerly stepping around and over the bodies of her customers.

"As soon as I saw Elaine, my heart went out to her. Here was a retiring, delicate, refined lady trying to teach the crude palates of this hardworking group an appreciation of squid salad and fried zucchini.

"A hopeless enterprise, and later, while she stuffed the night's meager take into a lush expanse of bosom, I offered her a way to save her struggling saloon.

"'First,' I said, 'you need some sensitive types in here.'

"'You mean fags?' she asked, her face colored by a gentle blush.

"'No,' I answered, 'I mean writers.'

"Elaine greeted this proposal with a quaint Jewish obscenity, so

Sonnet to Elaine

When in disgrace with luck and critics' eyes,
I all alone beweep my outcast state,
And trouble deaf agents with my bootless cries
And hate the way I look, and curse my fate,
Wishing me like to one with Chorus Line.
Solvent like him, like him with Cats *possessed,*
Desiring this man's Evita *and that man's* Nine,
With what I most admire contented least;
Yet in these thoughts myself almost despising,
Haply I think on thee, and then my state,
Knowing thou'lt smile and seat me well, starts rising
From Doll's Life *gloom, and I rush to thy gate;*
For thy Good *table to remembered such wealth brings,*
That then I scorn to change my state with kings.
—Betty Comden

I quickly explained to her the relevant virtues of my profession.

"'What would you say to some steady customers who don't have to get up in the morning and can therefore be plied with drinks until closing time? Who will eat anything put in front of them—and enjoy it?'

"Now there was a flicker of interest in her eyes.

"'Do they spend?' was her circumspect question.

"'An indifference to money is the hallmark of the profession,' I answered with pride.

"'Okay,' said Elaine, 'bring me a dozen.'

"I was surprised that she presented me with a bill when I headed for the door. Patiently, I explained to her that writers preferred the trust implied in the running up of tabs to the rude transactions of immediate payment. I then signed the back of the check, added a generous tip, and walked out into the night. From the warmth of Elaine's farewell words, I knew a lasting friendship had been formed."

T*he early Elaine's was, as Richardson says, a raucous,* brawling, hardscrabble saloon, and to keep even a semblance of order Elaine ruled with an iron fist, flinging brawlers into the street, pursuing check beaters, backing down from no one, a pugilistic trait she maintained throughout the years right up to the present day, her right-hand haymaker as lethal as ever.

"The first time I went to Elaine's was in 1967," the director Robert Altman says. "I walked in and there was a very rowdy table up in the front and Elaine was at her station by the bar. One of the guys at the table was making a ruckus with the waiter; the guy was wearing a scarf and Elaine came up behind him, grabbed him by the scarf and twisted it around his neck, yanked him up out of his chair, and threw him out the front door into the street. I knew then and there that this was my kind of place, and that I ought to make friends with that lady."

Elaine still asserts her authority physically, as she did recently in settling a dispute with an ambassador to the UN. "He's from some cockamamy country I never heard of," she says, "the check comes—he raises hell, says he won't pay the tax because he's got this tax-exempt card he sticks in my face. I shove the card away, and tell him loud and clear that *everybody* pays tax in Elaine's. His highness then tells me to shove the check up my kazoo, or words to that effect, and I blister him with a word or two which he's never heard from a lady before, and he torches me with some nasty foreign stuff, and I'm ready to clock him when big Frank Waters, who works the bar here, gets between us and stretches out his big arms like this, to keep us apart, but I come running under his arm and cold-cock the ambassador with a solid right that sends him skidding across the floor from bar stool three to bar stool seven. That'll teach him how not to talk to a lady. But Liz Smith makes an item of it, giving the impression that I'm the Mike Tyson of Second Avenue, which is simply not the case. Look, this is a late-night saloon and occasionally it's necessary to assert myself when things get a little out of hand. Actually my place is pretty genteel but by the nature of them, night places are prone to commotion, arguments, and physical demonstrations. For instance, that big window in back of me that's been broken three times: First when the playwright John Ford Noonan was kicked out of here because he was pestering Geraldo Rivera, who was at dinner with friends. Pissed at being outside looking in, John reared back and punched a big hole in the window, which at that time was made of heavy plastic. Then there was a guy who had a sizzling argument with his girlfriend, stormed out of here, seized a garbage can on the sidewalk, and threw it through the window, which was then made of glass. The last time, Bruce Jay Friedman, who wrote *A Mother's Kisses*, was coming in and got accosted by a drunk at the bar here, and the drunk got belted so hard his head hit the window and cracked it in two."

There is something definitely combustible about the atmosphere at Elaine's. The novelist Dan Greenburg recalls the time "an out-of-town friend was eager to be taken to Elaine's. She wanted to see the celebrity fistfights, she said. We assured her there were no such things. She knew better.

"We took her to Elaine's and got a table with some people we knew. Shortly after our arrival, two of the largest men I have ever seen walked in with a bimbo, and they sat down at the table opposite ours. It quickly became apparent that these folks had never been to this restaurant before, and that their idea of an effective way to get great service at Elaine's was to be loud and abusive and insult the waiters.

"Nobody waited on them. They became louder and more abusive. They were earnestly asked to leave, and they responded with picturesque figures of speech.

"The oversized gents kicked over a table and shouted an invitation to fight anybody in the place. A feisty young female journalist at our table announced that her table would take on their table. I hastily made it clear that this offer applied only to her and was void for her tablemates.

"The cops arrived. A scuffle ensued. Screams and blows were exchanged. Bruisers and bimbo were bum-rushed outside, where Ron Galella took flash pictures.

"Everybody was very excited. Everybody was very surprised. Everybody but our out-of-town friend—this was what she had known it was like. This was what she had come to see. We assured her that nothing quite this dramatic had happened at Elaine's in years.

"Our friend just smiled. She knew better."

When I first came back from Paris, to become publisher of *Women's Wear Daily*, at the end of 1964, the young fashion writers on the paper told me Elaine's was the place to go. It's cheap, they said, and the designers and the models all go there. We had an apartment a few blocks away, and we began to go there. It was for us then a neighborhood hangout. I have been going there since, perhaps eighteen hundred or two thousand nights. In all that time, Woody has spoken to me twice.

I don't know who it was who first said, "At Elaine's, all the girls are five-feet-nine and all the men are suntanned," but he had something.

When I went to work for Rupert Murdoch, two of his Australian reporters and I went to dinner there. George Viles hung his raincoat on a hook over Dick Avedon's head. Elaine snatched the coat off the hook. "Find someplace else to hang your coat than on Mr. Avedon's head," she advised. That same night, George and Steve Dunleavy arm wrestled at the table. Dunleavy said, "Brady has been building up his credit here for ten years and we've destroyed it in one night."

—JAMES BRADY, novelist

" The admirable thing about a writer is that he is doing what he wants to do. So many people are not doing what they want to do—not even close. So for that, writers get an automatic ten points. Sometimes a writer's book is a success, hits the bestseller list, his next book may be ignored, rejected, disappears without a trace, but the really good writers, success or failure, go right on to the next because they are not permitted the grace of imperfection. I mean, either you have talent or you don't have talent. A good writer's talent does not depend on the outcome of any one particular book. Publicity and success have nothing to do with each other. They're two separate entities. Some of my writers go ten years without a book, but I know when they are in my place, no different one year to the next, that they are exercising their talent every day. The stopwatch is for track, not for writers. "

—ELAINE

Everyone Comes to Elaine's

2

Writer William Styron

PHOTOGRAPH BY JESSICA BURSTEIN

By the mid-sixties, Elaine's had become virtually a writers' club. Elaine kept all her reservations for them, and late arrivals would be accommodatingly squeezed in with early squatters. I used to be there three or four nights a week at a table with Gay Talese, David Halberstam, the writer Michael Arlen, Jack Richardson, the *Esquire* editor Robert Brown, Bruce Jay Friedman, George Plimpton, Lewis Lapham, Peter Maas, and sometimes Norman Mailer. Most of us had not yet started writing books. Talese and Halberstam were unsalaried refugees from the *New York Times*, Plimpton had not yet played quarterback for the Detroit Lions, and I was living in a one-room fifth-floor walk-up, trying to write a book about Ernest Hemingway. But Elaine treated all of us royally. You paid when you could, and if you couldn't, you would someday when, you hoped, the work in progress hit the bestseller list.

"There had been forerunners," David Halberstam recalls. "Bleeck's for the *Trib* and *Times* people, when there was still a *Trib*, and *Times* people still lived in Manhattan. That is, a place where writers and reporters could go after work and continue to talk and argue shop, anything to do in the descending loneliness of postwork hours but go home. In the sixties, Elaine's became the place for many of us. In 1967, I left the *Times*, and then, more than ever, cut off from the informal club that a newspaper represents, for in a city room you are always surrounded by both friends and enemies; I was drawn to Elaine's.

"Later, people called it a literary salon. Perhaps, but though a lot of good writers made it their base, I can hardly remember a serious literary conversation. Instead it was almost all shoptalk, filled with the heat of ambition of young men, and a handful of young women,

Writers George Plimpton and David Halberstam

who were unwilling to let go of their professional dreams at six P.M. Mostly the talk was about money and royalties and sales and agents; when I first went there, the hot agent was Candida Donadio, and the hot editor was Bob Gutwillig, then of New American Library, who was said to be throwing around advances of twenty-five thousand dollars, and had even paid, it was said, forty thousand for a two-book contract. A man clearly loose with publishers' money.

Within the club that Elaine's was becoming, there was an Inner Club, table four, that is four tables down from the door. Norman Mailer and Jack Richardson held forth there, and admittance was with their approval, or with that of Elaine herself; if you were accepted by them you could sit down, or if Elaine brought you over and introduced you, you could sit down. Richardson was writing a book on gambling, and on occasion, late at night, turned the table into a poker table. Everyone who came was supposed to have achieved certain credentials. Only one person had not, a young kid named Frank Conroy, who kept telling everyone that he was writing his autobiography. He was brash and full of his own work, and since he had published *nothing*, his brash opinions on everything irritated a few of us. Then *Stop-Time* came out, and the rest of us bowed to his judgment; he *was* a writer.

"No one talked much about the books themselves nor, even though those years were politically charged, about politics. If there was a hot subject in the late sixties, it was not Vietnam—it was the Knicks. Suddenly people's eating habits changed: Instead of arriving at eight-thirty or nine P.M. they began coming in at ten-fifteen, right after the Knicks games. The only time I ever saw the celebrity-jaded atmosphere of Elaine's stilled (after all, we were used to Jackie O., Norman M., Yevtushenko, Gene McCarthy) was when Walt Frazier, then at the height of his fame with the Knicks, walked in. The place became silent. I mean absolutely *silent*."

"I was waiting tables that night," says Carlo Torchio, who has been with Elaine since the beginning. "Walt Frazier pulled up right in front of the restaurant in a brand-new white Rolls-Royce, a gorgeous woman with him. He gets out of the car, he is wearing a long mink coat with a matching mink fedora. As he goes to open the door for the lady, he notices that raindrops have left little marks on the hood of the Rolls, and he takes off his mink coat and uses it to polish the hood, then puts it back on, and helps the lady get out of the car."

The problem with pilot fish is that, true to their name, they lead other fish into their waters, namely sharks and barracudas, and that's what happened to Elaine's: Where there are writers, the sharks of Hollywood are sure to follow, for producers and directors need writers the way Elaine's kitchen needs calamari. The influx of these big Hollywood fish caused Elaine to enlarge and spruce up her narrow place, doubling, then tripling its size.

But it stayed crowded, because the big Hollywood fish attracted the glitter fish—the stars who feed off producers and directors the way producers feed off writers. Once all that was in place, it was inevitable that the gawker fish would come clamoring for tables, but Elaine stood at the gate, and only the select few were allowed in to swim with the glitter fish, the sharks, and the pilot fish.

It was at this point that Elaine's began to develop its snobby mystique: If you didn't know Elaine, she would keep you standing at the bar while her pets paraded by you on their way to the choice tables. Elaine's had become a New York institution, where one yearned to go but was afraid of venturing in as an outsider.

"Sometimes those outsiders give you a certain amount of trouble about it," says Nora Ephron, who wrote *Heartburn*. "'I suppose you're one of those people who go to Elaine's,' they say, and they look at you in a faintly disapproving way that implies that you have no values whatsoever.

"Sometimes I say: Look it's just a saloon that saves its best tables for writers, and then the writers write about it, so everyone thinks it's a big deal, but it isn't, really.

"Sometimes I say: It's like going to a dinner party where you don't quite know who's going to be there and you don't really have to talk to anyone except the person you came in with but at least you feel you've *been* somewhere, which is not a bad feeling when you've spent the day pretty much alone at the typewriter and suspect you haven't been anywhere at all.

"Sometimes I say: The truth is there aren't that many restaurants that are open late and don't mind if you take hours and hours over a meal.

"Sometimes I say: Listen, the veal chop is terrific.

"What I always mean to say is: You bet your sweet ass I go to Elaine's. I love it there. You wanna make something of it?"

Elaine maintains that all this is a misperception of her establishment, which, she claims, is as equitable as any other popular restaurant. "We honor reservations," she says, "and if you have booked a table, you get seated. But people who walk in off the street without reservations have to take their chances, like they do

The only time I ever saw the celebrity-jaded atmosphere of Elaine's stilled . . . was when Walt Frazier, then at the height of his fame with the Knicks, walked in . . . wearing a long mink coat.

PHOTOGRAPH BY JESSICA BURSTEIN

at other restaurants. As for certain tables going to my regulars, listen, I like having steady customers—it's my neurosis about being separated. I don't like people who just pass through and eat a meal to take a look. No voyeur from Scranton, concealing an instant camera, is going to be given a table, thereby putting Woody Allen or Clint Eastwood or Dustin Hoffman in jeopardy. My family, my regulars, come before anyone else, and I make damn sure that they have a table when they come in. I myself don't have a family. I'm glad I don't—I can't handle family squabbles and feuds and all that ugly stuff. My restaurant family is different. I know exactly who

Revlon chief Ron Perelman and his wife, actress Ellen Barkin they are and how they are, and I know that, whatever happened that day, when I come into my restaurant my spirits will pick up. I care about these people who have been in my life for thirty, forty years, and being with them gives me a wonderful sense of belonging.

"Like the night I was closing up, around three in the morning, when there's a knocking on the door and it's Jules Feiffer and his wife."

My choicest memory," Feiffer says, "is of the night my play *Little Murders* opened for a short week on Broadway, closing five days later because the reviews that night said it must. Enraged, despondent, and cold sober after four hours of drinking, I arrived, with my wife, at Elaine's at two-thirty in the morning. The door was locked, but the window was lit, just barely. In the weak glow I saw Elaine closing up. I rattled the knob, I knocked. She came to the door. She let us in. She sat us down. She bought us a bottle of champagne. For the next hour and a half, we were in complete agreement on what sons of bitches the critics were."

"We sat there sipping champagne," Elaine says, "with Jules firing bullets at the critics, sonsabitches this and that, and I'm being very sympathetic: You're right, Jules, sonsabitches who secretly hate the theater, fall asleep, are frustrated playwrights, and I'm carrying on for Jules, but actually I've got nothing against critics and I usually go to the plays they like, but for one of my writers who's hurting, they're all sonsabitches who can't get it up."

Elaine may think that she does not have family squabbles and feuds, but she has had her share of them. One case in point is the night Norman Mailer came in for a late dinner with a feisty young woman who was on a power trip because of the "name" she was with. The woman complained about their table, the scarcity of waiters, and that there was too much light, whereupon she reached up and unscrewed the bulb in the overhead fixture, a cardinal sin in Elaine's Book of Etiquette. Elaine went over and rescrewed the bulb. She was particularly sensitive about those bulbs, which were the first things she bought when she moved in. She got them from a store in the Village for five dollars each. They were mortuary bulbs. A couple seconds later, the woman unscrewed it again. Once more Elaine put the light back on, but right away, it got unscrewed, whereupon Elaine laid on Mailer's date a ton of invective she had never heard before. Mailer was screaming, "I don't need this! I don't need this! Knock it off! Cut it out!"

"I screwed on the bulb emphatically," Elaine says, "and as I was turning away from her, this ditsy broad hit me with her elbow, gives me a whack, so I spin around, but my hand was in the way, so it must have hit her when I spun and knocked her down. Whereupon she calls me a big, fat bully. 'Listen, sweetheart,' I say to her, 'get your ass outa here—him I have to take it from, but no half-a-hooker is going to fuck with my lightbulbs.'"

"The next day I received a really nasty handwritten note from Mailer—something like, You elephantine colossus, that carnage last night, slugging that poor defenseless girl—but I just wrote BORING, BORING, BORING right across it in big letters and sent it back to him. Mailer stayed away for a couple of years—I guess he thought he was punishing me—but then he came in for dinner one evening with friends and announced that from then on we were going to be as sweet and tender to each other as a couple of Chinese mandarins, whatever the hell that means."

I rattled the knob, I knocked. . . . She let us in . . . bought us a bottle of champagne. For the next hour and a half, we were in complete agreement on what sons of bitches the critics were.

In 1971, Gael Greene, food maven of New York *magazine, emphasized Elaine's position in the restaurant firmament:*

THE INTENSE INEVITABILITY OF ELAINE'S has survived the tensility of Mere Chic. I suspect it has gone beyond even the boundaries of Ritual Masochism. When Suzy designated Manhattan's seven "Beautiful People Restaurants," there, nestled amid all the obvious La's and Le's, was . . . Elaine's, with its antlers and deer heads and the ambiguous murky murals—is it the Rape of the Sabine Women or getting-to-know-you at the Woodstock Festival?

Elaine's: playpen of the quality media set. Salon *littéraire.* Reputations soar or stub mortally on how long a man has to stand at the bar of this lovingly seedy little joint on the Eighty-eighth Street edge of Nowhere before getting a table somewhere in the back of playwright Jack Richardson's head. "In" quotient like Elaine's does not stand impregnable without an iron will fighting back the riffraff, the gawking nobodies, the camping piranhas, and unamusing gypsy moths who could so easily clutter up the dining room and strain the loyalty of the pets *de la maison.* All this began with a poet or two, an off-Broadway playwright, and a few actor boozehounds. Elaine Kaufman is incurably taken by things literary. Everybody wants to be Somebody, and Elaine's Somebodies were mostly Nobody to Anybody Else.

Well, granted . . . clearly George Plimpton is as disarmingly adorable at the very tony Raffles as he is to Elaine. But what glacial maitre d' is likely to court Willie Morris? . . . How many *haut* snobberies will even recognize Gay Talese? Your average everyday groupie is not too likely to faint in religious ecstasy over the nearness of *Harper's* magazine's Lewis Lapham.

SO ELAINE'S IS ESSENTIAL. Writing is hell. A slow day at the typewriter is like a week in solitary. "It's solace to be there," *Life's* Tommy Thompson once observed, "and see the competition goofing off, nursing blocks . . ." And after the journalists, the editors, the playwrights, and actors came the pretty girls, celebrity collectors, moneyed sycophants, or class, artful appreciators . . . for what is an ego without a mirror? It would be a fatal bore if everyone in the room were a celebrity and no one a fan. But your peers make the best fans . . . at least, they don't do anything embarrassing, like steal your cuff links or ask for an autograph. And with the Manhattan Success Aristocracy outdazzling the blocked and undiscovered came Jackie in giant shades and, inevitable bliss, the Movie Stars, humbled in the presence of the Muses' many messengers. If Norman Mailer is here, can Raquel Welch be far behind? The crush grew Hieronymus Boschesque about the time Susan Stein and the Beautiful Burdens stopped giving so many parties. Or do I imagine it? If you wanted to keep in touch . . . see all your chums . . . you had only to drop by Elaine's. Anytime from twilight till four A.M. . . . guaranteed good gossip and good fettuccine . . . or as faithful Jackie Rogers put it: "A few giggles and a couple of fights."

Divorces were crueler. The parting two would calmly give up offspring, the Rothkos and the Poonses, the flat at

Some nights the turnover of fashionable ex's and about-to-be-ex's with soon-to-be-mates was dizzying.

the Dakota, but neither was willing to surrender custody of Elaine's. Some nights the turnover of fashionable ex's and about-to-be-ex's with soon-to-be-mates was dizzying.

And here is China Machado, dazzling beauty in African capelet, and Eve Orton in her body stocking. Muriel Resnik stalks the reservation disguised as an Iroquois squaw. Here are Michael Arlen, Jack Gelber, and the *Times*'s Arthur Gelb. Rita Gam in a prioress hood. The Dustin Hoffmans . . . Jack Nicholson five nights in a row. Bobby Short. Here is Nureyev embracing Roman Polanski . . . Nureyev came straight from the airport with suitcase in tow. David Frost, Diahann Carroll, Art Buchwald, and the Robert Mitchums, all on the same glorious night. Joe Namath insists on the back room. Rod Steiger and Tammy Grimes suffer exile with dignity. Antonioni and the Henry Fords.

When Mummy and the Duke of Bedford come into town, where else would daughter Caterine Milinaire throw her little supper? Naturally, Charlotte toasts baby brother Edsel's twenty-first birthday with fettuccine, veal piccata, endive, and cherries jubilee for sixteen. From the neighborhood come Christopher Cerf, Dan and Nora Greenburg, and Mayor John Lindsay. Then in walks the former mayor. "Look, it's Robert Wagner," someone cries. "Oh," says Lindsay, "I thought it was the Sundance Kid."

Success has given Elaine floor-length sables, a town house, and, recently, the building at 1703 Second. But she is still the penultimate fan. She has read the book. She has seen the show. She knows what everyone is up to, Herb Sargent notes, "She really listens." And she cares. *New York*'s

Writers William Styron, Frank Conroy, and Irwin Shaw

puzzle-poser Mary Ann Madden, having confessed a mad passion for Donald Sutherland, was deeply touched when Elaine phoned her at home one night. "He's here," was all Elaine said. Mary Ann threw on some clothes, leaped into a cab, and arrived at Elaine's half zipped. "She had neglected to say he was having dinner with Jane Fonda. I turned around and went home."

One evening some of the stalwarts were sitting around the Training Table and someone said, "Why don't we go somewhere else once in a while, instead of sitting here with all these people?"

The response has a solipsist finality. "Because," someone said, "*we are* all these people."

I ate at Elaine's every night for about ten years. With very few exceptions. It was always packed, high energy, and full of people I knew. Even on nights when it was zero degrees out it was jammed. I've eaten alongside everyone from Don King to Simone de Beauvoir. There was no celebrity that didn't show up there. It was fun to people-watch. I rarely spoke to anyone not at my table and never table-hopped. Rod Steiger kissed me on the lips once as I was walking out and a female in the movie business pinched me on the behind saying that even though she was a stranger to me she'd always wanted to do it. I never picked up a girl, although beautiful women were always there.

I played late-night-into-early-morning poker there with other writers and won some reasonable cash.

Elaine was always a wonderful friend—always there when anyone needed her. I was at her wedding (not the ceremony) party at the Carlyle Hotel and she made me feel that I could always count on her. I filmed at Elaine's several times and there were times I was the only customer in the place eating lunch. Elaine was a supporter of mine since my days as a stand-up comedian and has always been high on my films. One anecdote gives you her personality in a nutshell and better than pages of description.

Wanting to give me a compliment, she said she had seen my movie at a screening and had exchanged some nice words about it with Fellini, who came there to eat the one night that I was not there but playing jazz. She compared the work of the two of us, and I said with no false modesty that Fellini was a truly great artist as a filmmaker and that I was not comparable, to which she replied (trying to make me feel good), "Don't worry, you're creeping right up his ass."

—WOODY ALLEN

Who is this autocrat of celebrity dining, this arbiter of who hobnobs with whom? She is not an alumna of the Cornell restaurant school, nor did she apprentice at the Four Seasons, nor does she have a certificate from the Cordon Bleu. The celebrated novelist Irwin Shaw had this perception of her:

"Whom the gods adore they first make plump and equip with a curly smile, a twinkling, welcoming eye in which, almost hidden, lurks the steely calculation of a riverboat gambler and the nerve of a cat burglar. The gods free their favorites, in this case Elaine, from all sentimentalities of democracy, and by instinct furnish them with the invaluable, arbitrary snobbish gift of choosing favorites who rely only upon their own taste in such delicate matters. They often then find for them disreputable quarters in dilapidated and unfashionable parts of town and teach them how to keep potential patrons clamoring outside the door while a sea of empty tables awaits within. Sworn professional enemies are admitted gladly, to liven up the late nights and early mornings with accusation and invective, and booze flows freely to keep the clamor at its utmost height. The lady in question then carves herself into a more gracious shape, so that her hug is no longer an overwhelming tidal wave of affection and approval but a motherly caress. She also reads, knowing that an unread writer can empty a lively room in ten seconds flat.

"Bohemian herself, as she pretends her clientele is, she disdains such mundane things as numbers on a menu and uses tarot cards to make up her bills. The food is hearty, because she goes along with the delusion of her clients that they are hardworking men in need of sturdy nourishment. She has no need of flattery—her tastes are catholic, and the people she lets into her den she actually likes and enjoys. She is unflappable and serene among the throng, half of whom have visited their psychiatrist that day with tales of suicide, failure, and sibling hatred.

"She is an institution who refuses to become institutionalized. No pity is ever expressed; she never says, 'Time, gentlemen, please.' She knows that the first night you are in town, from no matter what quarter of the globe you have come, you must pay the ceremonial visit to the uptown Queen of the Night. At the busiest hour there is always one more chair ready for the poor devil who has just finished the first act of his play or been locked out of his apartment by his wife."

She knows that the first night you are in town, from no matter what quarter of the globe you have come, you must pay the ceremonial visit to the uptown Queen of the Night.

Elaine Kaufman *was born in Manhattan at 140th* Street and Amsterdam Avenue, and she embodies the humor and toughness and street smarts of a prototypical New Yorker. She is a large woman who has battled obesity all her life. "But when I was very young," she says, "I had the opposite problem—I was very skinny and I had rickets, which exasperated my mother who was a good cook and got angry with me because I was such a finicky eater."

Her sister Edith, thirteen years older, remembered that "the problem was that Elaine just didn't like to eat, which infuriated our mother, who like all Jewish mothers liked to have her children well stuffed with her good cooking. But Elaine just wouldn't eat. I'd watch my mother pinch Elaine's cheeks together, forcing her mouth open, and then shove food in her like you stuff a goose, you know, force-feed her. So Elaine had to eat to please our mother. Probably why she got so heavy later on. But as a little girl she was very friendly,

Elaine, age four

always smiling, happy. When she was in kindergarten the teacher told my mother she had a very unusual little girl and that she should expect great things from her."

"My father had a small dry goods store on Amsterdam Avenue," Elaine says. "It was the middle of the Depression, business fell off, so in the dead of night they backed a truck up to the store, loaded it up, and we moved to South Jamaica, Queens, on Sutphin Boulevard, where we lived in back of a much smaller store. That's where I grew up, back of the store."

"Elaine was always disappearing," Edith recalls, "and we'd have to comb the neighborhood looking for her. Four, five years old, she was out of the house."

"There was always this battle going on with my mother over this eating thing," Elaine says. "She'd shove food in my mouth, I'd spit it out. I think she was embarrassed that I was so skinny and rickety, and people might think it was her fault, not feeding me. The doctor said if I had my tonsils out I would start to eat, but when that didn't work, they put me in the hospital with no explanation. It made me afraid that they were going to get rid of me. So when I came back, to avoid being put back in the hospital, I ate what my mother fed me. It all became related to acceptance.

"My father was no problem, a sweet man, ruined by the Depression, all the life gone out of him, sitting in the parlor reading *The Jewish Forward*. Montgomery Ward opened in Jamaica and that put the last nail in the coffin. He got a job working nights in a food market, which he had no feeling for, but he'd come home with avocados in his pockets which we had never seen before. Also, we had never seen a steak. My mother never told me we were poor. I thought everyone ate beef liver like we did."

"I think one of the reasons the business failed," Edith says, "is the way my mother treated customers. If someone was looking at two, three things, taking her time making up her mind, my mother would wait only so long and then shout at the woman, 'Do you know what you want? If not, get out!' I guess that's where Elaine got the business of throwing certain people out of her place."

Four, five years old, I'm always out somewhere. To this day, I don't like homes, not even my own.

B
eing the youngest," Elaine says, "I was the one that everyone had to take care of. The reason I spent most of the time as a little kid running away from the house was I didn't like it at home. Four, five years old, I'm always out somewhere. To this day, I don't like homes, not even my own. In the business world, people are much nicer to each other because they hold the manners. In the house I grew up in they didn't seem to hold the manners in exchanges with each other. I guess I eventually fell into business because there are rules and everybody abides by them. It's much easier. I had a lot of friends in the Italian neighborhood where we lived. They'd invite me in and I got to know the food. The Italian mothers would let me make pastas with them, and I picked up some Italian words. I wasn't doing much at school, I never liked school, but I loved to read and I was really educating myself with books. My brother, who was about five years older, if he went to the library he had to take me. So he'd leave me in the

children's section. I'd read, and afterward I would bring a bunch of books home. I read them all."

Edith says that "one of the big frictions between my mother and Elaine was over school. I liked school and I was good at school but Elaine wasn't. She wanted to be out of the house, no home-work, and my mother couldn't understand. Why don't you get grades like Edith does? Elaine didn't want any part of it."

"I didn't get an allowance but I always had some money," Elaine says. "When we had the cash register in the front of the store my brother and I knew how to pilfer the tax money. Also, I used to go to the store for the women who lived on the second and third floors. They'd throw me down the money and the shopping list, and I'd go get it, bring it up, and they'd give me a quarter. Or they'd pay me to watch babies outside the front of the house. I wanted to get out of that house. It wasn't nice there. I mean, every season there were new slipcovers and there were

E*laine's was only a few months old* when Willie Morris, then a young subeditor at *Harper's*, lured me there on the pledge I might meet my literary betters: George Plimpton, Norman Mailer, Jack Richardson, Gay Talese. Alas, we didn't run into anybody more exciting than Dan Jenkins and David Halberstam. And I already knew them.

In time, however, I would meet at Elaine's all the writers Willie prom-ised and many, many more. Only about twenty percent proved to be ass-holes. This is much more tolerable than the national average.

—LARRY L. KING, writer

Here Is My "Top Ten List" of Things I Have Heard Elaine Say

10. You just get up every day and give it another shot.

(*On the secret of her success.*)

9. They're like checks in a drawer waiting to be cashed.

(*Comforting a writer who had written several things that hadn't sold.*)

8. Anybody else would have made it a weekend.

(*To a male customer upset about the end of a long relationship.*)

7. He never disappoints you.

(*On seeing a customer behave badly.*)

6. On my worst day . . .

(*Said with disdain when someone asked her if she ever had a happy hour.*)

5. I don't care who your father is.

(*To two very young girls who protested when Elaine wouldn't let them in the bar.*)

4. You wouldn't know an actor if you tripped over one.

(*To an arrogant film producer who was badmouthing actors.*)

3. Write.

(*To a writer who asked Elaine how he could overcome his writer's block.*)

2. Why is this night different from all other nights?

(*To a customer who walked in on Passover and was surprised she wasn't closed.*)

And the number one thing I heard Elaine say is . . .

1. Getting a table here is a memory for you.
(*To a customer who really annoyed her.*)

—CHARLES KIPPS, writer and producer

new curtains and all that kind of crap. I barely graduated from Evander Childs High School, it was so boring. I used to read the *Daily News* underneath the desk, and whatever held, held. I got just enough grades to get through.

I told my mother I wasn't going to be like the other girls. I wasn't going to work in an office, and I wasn't going to marry a nice boy.

"I started not turning up at home when I was sixteen or seventeen, and I split as soon as I could—I guess I was about eighteen. I didn't know what I had in mind. I told my mother I wasn't going to be like the other girls. I wasn't going to work in an office, and I wasn't going to marry a nice boy, because I didn't have anything to say to people like that. 'What are you talking about?' she said, and she hit me. When they don't know what you're talking about, right away they attack. I told my mother I wouldn't get married her way, to a nice quiet boy. I like the esoteric—a writer, a painter, somebody like that. Their thinking is freer. They see more than one shape in a form. How could my mother have understood that? She ran away from Russia when she was a young girl. Can you imagine how it was then? Now it's nothing—an airplane trip. Then it was steerage for three weeks or a month to get here. Now that was women's lib when it took guts. Especially since it was her lover she ran away with. Can you imagine? She didn't marry him—my father came later. I guess I've got some of her genes.

"There was no thought of college, girls didn't go to college where I came from, boys went to college, but I had no idea what I wanted to do. My mother expected me to work in an office like my sister, secretarial work, but I didn't like office work because I didn't like being enclosed. I got a job at Brunswig and Fils in the cutting room, where they cut the swatches to show fabric. I did that for a while until they found out I was Jewish, and they fired me. Nothing like that had ever happened to me before. I was more annoyed

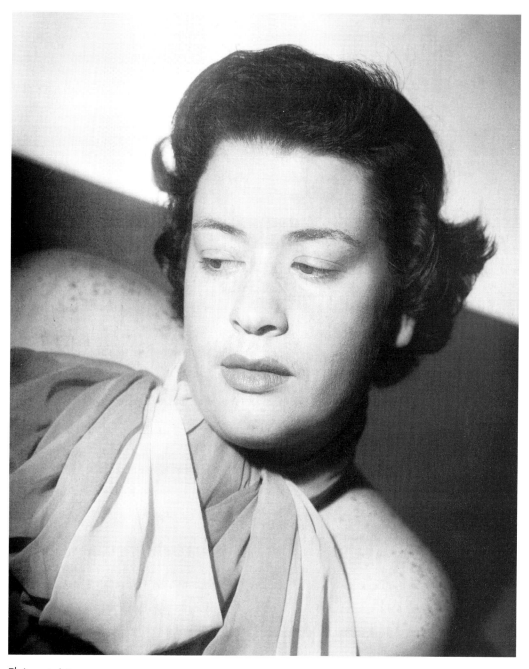

Elaine at sixteen

than angry. The guy who got my job was Italian. What's so great about that? The Italian neighborhood I lived in, they knew I was Jewish but it didn't matter.

"This was a period when I really expressed myself. I colored my hair with a spray, I had green bangs, I guess it was the influence of the beatniks, and I wore wonderfully crazy hats. I had all these meshugena hats with my green hair, and it was great! The next job I got was in the Stampezine, a famous stamp auction house and used bookstore in midtown Manhattan. President Franklin Roosevelt had been a big stamp collector and some of his were up for auction.

After that I decided to get a job selling cosmetics. I finagled a job at the Astor Hotel pharmacy; by the time they realized I didn't know anything, I knew something. Lou Costello would come in with a babe and he would buy her a Chanel lipstick, which was like five dollars, big deal, and then she would go upstairs with him and afterward come back down and want to trade in the lipstick.

"My friends and I started to take ballet lessons with Madame Chamier, who was above the Legett's store at Fifty-seventh and Seventh, and afterward we'd cruise all the Broadway shows, sneaking in at the intermissions and seeing the second acts. After the Astor, I got a traveling job selling L'Amour cream and curlers, going all the way to New Haven, but although I was good at making my spiel, my pitch, and attracting people, I was never able to get them to buy anything. I also had a job doing market research, going around with a clipboard and asking people questions about coffee, do you like this one or that one, and writing down their responses. They caught me filling out the questionnaires without asking anyone anything and I got canned—fucking stupid waste of money. I was then living at the Versailles Hotel on Sixtieth Street where they had tiny maids' rooms under the roof for ten dollars a week."

"It was at this point," Edith says, "with Elaine drifting around, that I took her to my analyst for an interview. Right off the bat he took her on and transferred me to his assistant. Elaine and I would go once a week and then on another day we'd meet with a group."

"Going to that shrink was my college," Elaine says.

"Late one night I was playing backgammon with Robert Altman and the superagent, Sam Cohn. I had a marvelous run of luck. The next day I took my winnings and bought a share in the *So-Ho News.*"

—ELAINE

Everyone Comes to Elaine's

4

Robert Altman and his wife

PHOTOGRAPH BY RON GALELLA

Despite the beneficial sessions with her analyst, Elaine was still floundering, scruffling from one meaningless job to another until the evening in Greenwich Village when she went to dinner with friends at an Italian restaurant called Portofino, where she found her calling. "When the Italian waiter comes to the table to take our order," Elaine says, "and he looks at me and smiles—glistening black hair, glistening black eyes, glistening white teeth—I feel like Katharine Hepburn meeting Rossano Brazzi in Rome.

"'I am your waiter,' he says with a divine accent. 'My name is Alfredo.'

"I am sitting there with a goopy look on my face. 'Alfredo,' I murmur."

"'Si, Alfredo Viazzo—what's yours?'

"'Elaine-o,' I say, dying to be Italian.

"'Elaine-o,' he says, 'you have the most beautiful green hair I have ever seen.' He says he's from Genoa, that he was a steward on a United States Line cruise ship but he jumped ship. I am tongue-tied. He recommends the gnocchi primavera. All my senses are percolating.

"I ate three lunches that afternoon and moved in with him two days later. To be near him, I decided to become a waitress. Alfredo Viazzo—my present from the Italian government—showed me how to wait tables, how to hold a plate, everything. I was a total ignoramus. I didn't even know how to put out the silver. I came from a home where the silver got put out on the table in a pile and everybody took what they needed. I gave it a try and found that waitressing was a perfect fit for me, my life's glove—it excited all the things I like to do: describing the food to make it interesting, getting a fix on the customer's moods, and then dealing with it so he enjoys himself, perking him up if he's had a rotten day, babying him with the menu if he needs it, amusing him if he's in a bantering mood. Everybody has a different need at a certain time, and I found that reading moods came natural to me. And so did Alfredo."

Cy Coleman, the Broadway composer, notably of *Sweet Charity* and *Barnum!*, says, "I've always felt that I deserve a special place on the long list of Elainophiles since I was one of the very first to know her and banter with her about the world at large and the state of practically everything. This was in the Village in an Italian restaurant off Bleecker Street, where Elaine was working. I was dating Sylvia Miles, the actress, who was appearing in Genet's *Balcony* at the Circle in the Square theater, which was right around the corner from the restaurant. There I discovered Elaine's talent to make you feel comfortable when you're alone at a bar waiting for the curtain to come down around the corner, which I did, night after night. Her amazing ability to talk about anything and also be an avid listener were the essential elements for the life that she was destined to create uptown."

I didn't even know how to put out the silver. I came from a home where the silver got put out on the table in a pile and everybody took what they needed.

"Alfredo and I had been working there a while when the guy who owned it, who really didn't dig the restaurant business, said to us, 'Why don't you buy it—you can pay it off.' So we did, and at first it went okay."

"I first met Elaine in the fifties," the nationally syndicated columnist Liz Smith says, "when she was waitressing at Portofino, a restaurant in the Village not far from where I then lived. Not only waitressing but running the place, which was ostensibly run by a charming Italian named Alfredo Viazzo, who was dashingly handsome but hopelessly detached. Elaine was exactly then as she is now—gruff, funny, full of New York wisdom, with an instinct for all the things a restaurant requires."

T*he restaurant was beginning to have a following* but Alfredo was bored with it, felt that he was destined for far greater things, and announced that he was going to add a little theater in the back and put on one-act plays and little musicals, which he would write and direct, so that for twenty dollars a head, customers could watch the play while they were eating. Elaine thought it was a rotten idea but Alfredo forged ahead. He took over the store next door, thereby enlarging the restaurant from eight tables to eighteen, and he signed a lease for a third store where he put the theater with tables that could accommodate an additional twenty. He got the leases from Mama Rosa, who was the moneylender in the neighborhood and who owned the stores.

"Where will you get these plays?" Elaine asked.

"I will write them. I am very strong in this."

"What about actors? They don't come cheap."

"I have friends not working. They will do it for the exhibition."

I *was friends with Alfredo," Carlo Torchio says. "I was a* waiter at another restaurant but I came to Portofino quite often. That's how I met Elaine. Alfredo was a great storyteller, a great ladies' man, and he could have been a great restaurateur—he was a terrific cook—but his mind was in theater and movies. He wanted

PHOTOGRAPH BY JESSICA BURSTEIN

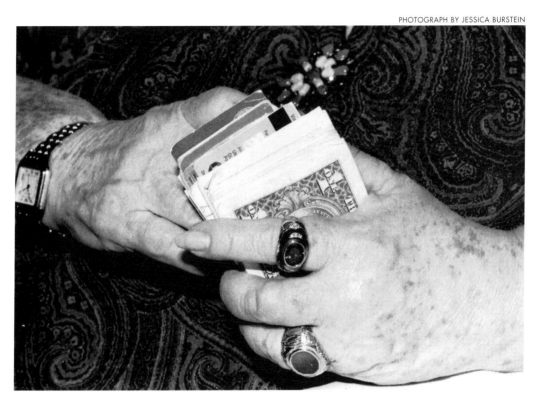

These are the rings that landed on the jaw that got Elaine in trouble with the law

to be a film producer, a writer, a director, he wanted to be a Fellini, a Bertolucci. He had big ideas. 'I'm wasting my time as a restaurateur,' he would say. 'I should be directing movies.' In the meantime, Elaine is totally running the restaurant, waiting tables, writing the checks, sweeping up, stocking the bar, ordering supplies, directing traffic, and he's giving orders, but as time went by Elaine became more and more like we know her today—independent, forceful, right in your face."

"I told him, 'Alfredo, this ain't working,'" Elaine says.

"'No, no, is working, they love us, they go out of here singing one of my songs.'

"'Yeah? Well, how come they never come back? The food is a helluva lot better than the fuckin' plays.'

"'Elaine, these things take time to build. I have surprise for you—I have got my divorce from my Italy wife, and now we can marry.'"

"'I would've, Alfredo, but I discussed it with my analyst and he talked me out of it. And he's right. The business is slowly going broke because you're takin' my money but you're not payin' off the notes. You could have bought this place in a year, all you had to do was pay the notes.'

"'You accuse me of not paying the notes?"

"'Yes, for the bimbo you've been seeing—spending all our money on her.'

"'Lie! You are a liar!'

"'And you are a four-flusher—look it up!'

"'And you are a *porchetta grassa*—look that up!'

"'Let me put it this way. What you can do with this restaurant— *va fa un culo, capiche?*'

"It was a slam-bam breakup fight—I smashed every glass and plate in the joint,, zing, zing, zing, pitched 'em against the walls, glass everywhere. Took my money—zing! Didn't pay the landlord—zing! Wrote lousy dialogue—zing! . . . zing! . . . zing! . . . zing!"

What I really don't like is to have to raise the price of something on the menu. Diane shows me the invoice on Dover sole, for instance, shows me how much they've gone up. I try to keep the increase at twenty-five cents, but Diane is always frustrated with that since that doesn't cover the increase. But I'm always afraid that the price will scare people off, stop them from ordering. From the beginning, I've wanted to keep prices at a level that working-class people could afford. I was preoccupied with that, so that young people wouldn't hesitate to come in, because they're interesting and they're learning and they're the future. But at the same time, I wanted top-quality ingredients and I wanted plenty of good service, so in the economics of things the prices on the menu had to be adjusted. We still get a lot of young people in here, but I worry about the ones who can't afford to come in.

—ELAINE

*S*ure, Elaine is the number one hostess of contemporary literature, but think what she could have done for Dostoevsky. His oeuvre lacked only one quality, namely jolliness, and that he would have learned at the pavilion of universal love that is Elaine's, where there's more embracing per square foot than at a girls' camp reunion, even though hugger has just robbed huggee of his percentage points of the producer's net. If Fyodor had steeped himself in some of that, how it would have brightened the texture of *The Brothers Karamazov*.

On the other hand, Elaine would have taught humility to Nietzsche: All she'd have had to do was point at Woody Allen, the establishment's resident Superman, who lives at a table far back and garlic-close to the kitchen.

Kafka would have refined his angst at Elaines'—especially after a Broadway opening night. That's when two chubby critics in dinner jackets enter the restaurant to be ushered to a spot next to Bobby Zarem. Examine them closely: They are the killers of Joseph K., "two plump, pallid, formally dressed men," sixty years later and alive and well at a good table. The pair, sipping their screwdrivers, would make a fine opening chapter for *The Trial II*.

Elaine's would have expanded the horizons of Donatien de Sade. The good marquis in his simplicity thought that the infliction of cruelty stimulated only sexual pleasure. But in this establishment, patrons stand in line for hours, waiting to be seated, being jostled by waiters, having wine spilled on them by hand-waving bar convivialists, being mistaken for Gene Hackman, all of which heightens the joy on their faces when at long last they are allowed to sit down and realize the pain and humiliation of the waiting line.

Last, not least, an evening at Elaine's would have been good for Homer. Correction, two evenings. By the end of the first evening, the bard would have been less blind: Getting the wrong check featuring three vodka martinis you never ordered makes a fellow sharp-eyed quick. And once he had had his cataract cured, Homer would have benefited on his second Elaine's evening by watching Gay Talese. Gay, getting up from his chair and setting sail for the men's room, embarks on an odyssey to the 'nth power. It's a voyage so wondrously labyrinthine in its table-hopping, so brilliant in its detours, so rich in swordplay and ingenuous laughter, so mythic in its encounters with archetypes, sex symbols, major gods, and minor demons, that Homer would have been much more of a mensch of an epicist just for the watching of it.

—FREDERIC MORTON, writer

" Right off the bat, I liked having writers around. They're a thinking group, and they're right out front with their feelings, and they're funny and intelligent. They like to stick together, because they're all under the same strain of working on their own against a blank piece of paper. But they don't talk about writing, because they've had that all day long, so they turn their minds to other things. And they keep the same hours. What good's a saloon for stockbrokers who watch the *Today* show while they're getting dressed? "

—ELAINE

Everyone Comes to Elaine's

5

Truman Capote, who was
turned away at the entrance

PHOTOGRAPH BY JESSICA BURSTEIN

A **fter her donnybrook bustup with Alfredo,** Elaine felt galvanized to find a place she could call her own, but with only a few thousand dollars to her name there would be no way for her to relocate in any of the good restaurant districts where restaurants went for fifty thousand on up. Besides that, she quickly discovered that no one wanted to do business with her.

"At that time women didn't run restaurants," she says. "They weren't supposed to know anything. All I was after was a nice place that would attract neighborhood people, and I figured if I ran it right I could make a living. That's all I was after. I knew I needed a partner who would put up half the money and lend a male presence to any negotiations. After a lot of desperate searching, I finally found a partner in Donald Ward, who owned a bar near Portofino. We each put up five thousand dollars—I had part of it and Edith lent me the rest. We went around to the brokers and found that a place at Eighty-eighth and Second was the only one we could afford, because the location was way beyond where people went to eat, and the Yorkville neighborhood where it was located didn't have a great reputation. It was working class—all those people who worked on Park Avenue, Madison, and Fifth—the doormen, the nannies, housekeepers, cooks. It was a German-Hungarian neighborhood, where the guys who worked in the subways and bus drivers all lived, had cheap rent, and this place I found, Gambrino's, was an Austro-Hungarian bar with eight kitchen tables, a place where the guys who lived in the neighborhood would come for a shot and a beer and a plate of whatever was cooked that day. They saved their money and then brought the family over. I left everything just as it was—the fixtures, the old paint, the bar.

We went around to the brokers and found that a place at Eighty-eighth and Second was the only one we could afford, because the location was way beyond where people went to eat.

"The first day I walk in as the new owner, the jukebox is playing a Bavarian folk song and a guy in a checked suit has set himself up at the telephone, a bookie taking bets. I feel like I'm in *Guys and Dolls*—'I've got the horse right here'—I give him a poke in the back.

"'Who the hell are you?' I ask.

"'I'm Jake. You're the new owner? Everything's Jake, sugar. Don't worry, you'll get the same vigorish.'

"'I get the same what? Vigorish? Sounds like a diet supplement.'

"'Forty bucks a day, sugar.'

Elaine's site was this wine shop before becoming Gambrino's

"'For what?'

"'The phone. I run a business—ten to three.'

"'Well, Jake, this sugar's gone sour and you just went out of business.'

"'All right, fifty, but that's it, sugar—no shakedown.'

"'Jake, get your bookie ass outa here.' He gives me the finger but he packs up his stuff and leaves.

"For weeks, Jake's customers kept calling. I pitched 'em to come in here for dinner, but I guess horseplayers don't eat, and save all their money for the track.

"I found a cook, an old guy, seventy-five, who was retired, and I pleaded, You've got to help me, you've got to help me. He finally took pity and worked the dinner hours. He made homemade pasta that he strung up on clotheslines all over the kitchen ceiling. You walked into the kitchen, you had pasta in your hair. The night I opened I looked around this dark, narrow place with its eight kitchen tables, and I said, Elaine, baby, you've got a long way to go."

Joe Allen *now has two very successful restaurants in* Manhattan's theater district, Orso and Joe Allen, and a clutch of restaurants bearing those names in Paris, Los Angeles, London, and Miami, but his beginning was as humble and tentative as Elaine's.

"At the time Elaine was starting at Portofino," Joe says, "I was getting my first job working for Danny Lavezzo who owned PJ Clarke's, a saloon-restaurant on Third Avenue at Fifty-fifth Street. Prior to connecting at those places, Elaine and I had both been living a clueless existence, neither of us had a defined interest in any pursuit, but when Danny suggested that instead of spending all my time drinking at the bar (I had a wad of severance pay from the army), I go to work for him as a bartender, it was a magical suggestion. Right off the bat I knew that restaurant life was a perfect fit for me. I didn't know that until I started to work there—just as Elaine fell in love with restauranting the minute she began waitressing at Portofino.

"We were both in awe of Danny, and we learned a lot from him.

E*laine's a very good business*-person. She won't leave here at night until she gets the register rung out, and the receipts in her hand, and the whole nine yards on what we did for the night. In fact, she can eyeball the room and tell you how much money we've done almost to a penny. She's unbelievable. She's the best. You work for Elaine Kaufman, you don't work for anybody else. Ask any of the waiters here. If you work here, she hired you. If she hired you, she knows what you're capable of and she leaves you alone. Another thing—we've carried a lot of guys here over the years. And every one of them has been a prince and paid their check. Some guys left a check for a month, two months, some guys for a year, sometimes three years. We had one guy here, buying Champagne, a Frenchman, buying Champagne like it was going out of fucking style. Back in the Studio Fifty-four days. And all of the sudden he disappears. Where is he? We don't know. What are we going to do with his checks? Now he comes back twelve, fifteen years later and pays the checks, and gives her a five-thousand-dollar bonus. We're talking thousands of dollars.

—TOMMY CARNEY, *Elaine's bartender for twenty-seven years*

Danny Lavezzo was truly eccentric as a businessman, and Elaine and I adopted many of his unorthodox ways, and it worked.

He was Mr. New York and New Yorkers loved him. Clarke's was a grimy place—dark, exposed brick walls, probably not painted since the First World War, the menu on a chalkboard on the back wall, the same dark, mellow feel that eventually predominated at Elaine's and at my first restaurant. But back there in the early sixties, Elaine and I weren't thinking about starting restaurants. We were just hanging on to our jobs, and we were both impressed with the clientele that Danny attracted to the back room. There was a packed noisy bar up front, but the rear was busy with celebrities— Buddy Holly proposed marriage there, and Aristotle Onassis was often there with Lee Radziwill in the years before he married Jackie Kennedy. Louis Armstrong would drop in early in the morning with his trumpet after performing at one of the jazz clubs. Nat King Cole was a regular—he anointed the bacon cheeseburger 'the Cadillac of burgers,' and table twenty-three was reserved for Frank Sinatra anytime he was in New York.

*T*here was one early evening, around five o'clock, lunch had cleared out and cocktails hadn't started, when Elaine was coming up to visit. We went into the back room and there, at separate tables, waiting for their guests, the only three people in the room were the mobster Frank Costello, Senator Hubert Humphrey, and Marilyn Monroe. All the time I was working there, late fifties, it seemed as though whoever was in the headlines that day was there that night, be it politicians, gangsters, movie stars— it didn't matter. It was magical. It was fun to go to work because there was all this stuff going on around you. Elaine knew about all this, we talked about it, that it was like going to the theater. In those days, people still drank until four in the morning, and you had to chase them out. It was a real honest-to-God saloon. At one point it was opening at eight in the morning, and closing at four. Then they'd sweep it up and throw down fresh sawdust, and here we'd go again. Who would have dreamed that eventually Elaine would repeat that scene once her place way uptown got up to speed?

"Danny Lavezzo was truly eccentric as a businessman, and Elaine and I adopted many of his unorthodox ways, and it worked. But when I decided to open up my own place—and he told the same thing to Elaine—he very seriously tried to talk me out of it. 'Look,' he said, 'I have all this success but you can't count on this

There's no denying that Elaine Kaufman is a force to be reckoned with. She's a large woman with an encyclopedic mind that jumps from one subject to another and a temperament not well suited to suffering fools. Her conversational style tends toward jumbled non sequiturs, yet she gets annoyed with anybody who fails to keep up. I remember one night when Elaine started telling me something about Argentina. At first I thought she was talking about a new wine she'd added to the list. But then she mentioned something about the Nazis, and I knew she'd lost me. I looked to a waiter for help, but he just shrugged and slunk away. It turned out Elaine was talking about the famous Nazi hunter Peter Malkin, who'd been in the restaurant the night before. "Don't you read?" she demanded angrily before stomping off.

—BRIAN MacDONALD, journalist and onetime Elaine's bartender

happening to you. This is a fluke thing and I'm having a good ride on this pony (Danny was an inveterate horseplayer), but the restaurant business is as chancy as a horse race and you're backing a nag with lousy odds. You're much better off with a real job. This life ain't for the likes of you.'

Of course, Elaine and I knew by then that it was sure as hell the life for us. We had learned that the mechanics, the nuts and bolts of the restaurant business, are not really rocket science. It's called paying attention. Elaine Kaufman has been where she is for so long, doing so well, because she pays attention almost every day. She's rarely not there. And she sees everything. Elaine and I are kind of the last of a particular generation. I can't think of anybody younger than we are who understands the age we're speaking of. I don't even know how to define it, but it was a different point of view. It was certainly, if nothing else, pre–rock and roll. The clubs today are totally different— they're not the kind of places that we frequented. A friend of mine was involved in looking for space for a disco, but all he wanted was a three-year lease because he knew that's the shelf life of a disco.

"When I tell Danny that, despite his misgivings, I'm going out on my own, he really explodes, 'You're crazy! At a time like this? You know the mortality rate for new restaurants in this city—enormous! Something like seventy-five percent don't last five years and lose their entire poke—in fact, wind up drowned in debt.'

"It made me doubt myself a little, but, I thought, I can't be this wrong. There's always gonna be some guy like me with a dream who makes it. Elaine went through the same thing a couple of years later. In my case, I found a partner, scouted the market, and wound up with the only place we could afford at Seventy-third and Third. Called it Allen's. Now Seventy-third, in those days, you'd get a nosebleed going that far uptown. The El was down but they were just starting to build all those high-rises which, as yet, didn't have tenants who would eat at the local restaurants. It was kind of a wasteland. So imagine what it was like for Elaine when, a couple of years later, she opens her place on Eighty-eighth and Second. I remember when Malachy McCourt opened on Sixtieth and Third, two years before me, and everyone thought he was like a pioneer going west, only this was the drinking itinerary going north.

"Elaine came to my opening and supported me all the way. I had made my place a carbon copy of Clarke's—same dark interior, exposed brick, all that, the same look that Elaine would bring to her place. I knew she had busted up with Alfredo but I was concerned when she told me she had bought a place on Eighty-eighth and Second. Her partner was Don Ward, who was a friend of mine. I thought I had stretched the restaurant area to its limits, but Elaine was at the North Pole.

"Allen's did all right for a beginner, but I had a disagreement with my partner, gave up the location, and moved to where I am now, at Forty-sixth between Eighth and Ninth, in the theater district. Those first years both Elaine and I had a helluva struggle. Elaine even more than me. I went up there often, kind of like I felt I had an obligation to help keep her going. It was like the two of us were in a battle. Every day was the Alamo. We worried about everything. Paying our suppliers, the people working on the place, the help, everything was a worry. It's now 1965, pretty much pre–air conditioning, people away for the summer, theaters shut down, tourists not coming to hot New York, and, contrary to popular belief, things didn't pick up on Labor Day. People didn't start coming back, the city didn't really pick up, until the middle of October, and the difference between Labor Day and the middle of October—when there were bills to pay for the meat and the fish and the vegetables and the booze—was like five lifetimes, waiting for this thing to get going, when you only see a few fannies in those seats around those empty tables.

Elaine *was going through the same thing. We agreed* that basically what we had done was to buy ourselves a job, that we were never going to be rolling in money but that we would survive somehow or other. Restaurant buying is rather simple. You buy a certain amount, and if that's too much, the next time you buy less, and if it's not enough, the next time you buy more. It's not coming in by stagecoach, you know. You call up and it's delivered a day or two later. Elaine and I both had that philosophy.

"What provided Elaine with customers early on was her being sympathetic to writers. And that's how I got started—being sympathetic to dancers, which often meant that we had to carry them on the books when they were broke. I'd tell 'em to just sign the check. Elaine knew writers wanted to be in her place, I knew dancers wanted to hang out at Joe Allen, so that made them responsible. How many times they'd come in and say, Look, I know I owe you all this money and I'll pay it when . . . and I'd say, When you can. Just pay your rent first and then pay me. And what's incredible is that the amount of money I've lost on tabs all these years wouldn't get me to Florida on a bus. Same goes for

"OH, GOOD... ROOM JUST OPENED UP AT THE BAR..."

Elaine always manages to have a table for her regular customers, even if it means throwing somebody else out. One day my producer and I came back from location on *Buffalo Bill* and we walked into the restaurant without a reservation. "No problem," Elaine said, and promptly threw a couple out of the place. Well, they were furious, and as they walked past, one of them turned out to be my producer's sister.

—ROBERT ALTMAN, filmmaker

Elaine, I'm sure. But every night we were there, paying attention, listening to those who were becoming regulars, caring about them, knowing that they would some day make their mark."

Other than the elderly cook, Elaine had no employees; she washed the dishes, waited tables, tended bar, tabulated the checks, and swept the floor.

Those beginning days, Elaine would sit at the door in the morning and scrutinize the products as they arrived—the vegetable man with his boxes of salad, the meat supplier with a side of beef, the fishmonger with a crate of calamari, the dessert supplier with boxes of cake and macaroons. Elaine would inspect the offerings closely and then pay for them in cash, which she extracted from the large pocketbook she kept beside her. Other than the elderly cook, Elaine had no employees; she washed the dishes, waited tables, tended bar, tabulated the checks, and swept the floor.

"How we caught on was just luck," Elaine says. "Nelson Aldrich lived around the corner. He had just come back from Paris, where he'd been working on *The Paris Review* with George Plimpton and Fred Seidel, the poet. Nelson was teaching in a special school in Harlem, not far from the restaurant, and he walked by one night, came in for a drink. One after the other Nelson's writer friends came, and once the writers started coming they attracted publishers and actors, and now I'm getting more reservations than I can handle in my little place. One night a lot of people with reservations were waiting and getting very impatient, and I was crazed. I didn't know what to do—at Portofino people came, ate, and went off to the theater or the movies. But now they just sat and sat. I put the checks under their noses but nobody got up. So this night, crazed, I go into the kitchen and turn off the exhaust, smoke starts coming into the restaurant, then I come out and tell the people at the tables, I'm terribly sorry but there's a grease fire in the kitchen. I have the firemen coming, so I'll have to close up for a while. So they all left, we threw the exhaust back on, and I could seat the ones who were waiting.

"Opening my very own place, wanting to make a go of it, my goal just to make a decent living, I knew I had to learn the ropes right up front. I talked to owners and chefs who had a lot more expertise. I learned first, keep a control on the icebox, know what you have in your icebox. Don't prepare too much at a time—better to run out of a special than to have it run over. Seeing what people prefer and catering to tastes. It's all mathematics in a sense. You pay so much for your item, you pay so much for the cook to prepare it, the porter to clean up, the bartender . . . you know, it's subtraction and addition."

" The filmmaker Emile de Antonio was in here often. When I saw the documentary *Millhouse* I thought Emile had gone too far. I told him, 'Nixon can't be that bad.' Then Watergate happened. "

—ELAINE

Everyone Comes to Elaine's

6

Carl Bernstein
(*All the President's Men*)
at Willie Morris's book party
for *New York Days*

PHOTOGRAPH BY JESSICA BURSTEIN

Jules Feiffer, playwright, novelist, cartoonist, says, "Many of the type who, in Groucho's phrase, wouldn't belong to a club that would have them as members belong to Elaine's. It was, at root, a men's club for the literary lonely. In the early sixties, when I first attended, I found writers, journalists, and editors wandering in off the streets at night after their dinner parties, with or without spouses, eager at least to find someone to talk to.

"I slipped into the habit of confiding intimate portions of my life to people who were all but strangers outside the joint. Elaine turned us intimate. I confessed who knows what. Who could remember the next morning? What I remembered was the glow of specialness brought on by the knowledge that I had associates, colleagues, comrades—although I wasn't sure of some of their names. Their acceptance by Elaine was the guarantee of their legitimacy. On nights that I came in alone, she knew at which group's table I would fit. As the drinks multiplied, I hopped to other tables, sideswiping other drifters caught in the current, surfing the length of the room, stalking the big wave."

The big wave of regulars gave Elaine's a nightly aura akin to the writers' and dramatists' clubs of London.

"So now we're starting to do all right," says Elaine, "but I'm having trouble with my partner, Donald, who's supposed to be helping me but was spending all his time at the bar, drinking. When he did handle the door, which was his job, he was a disaster. One night Truman Capote came to the entrance and Don said, 'I'm not letting fags in here' and turned him away. Not long after that I bought off Don's share and we parted company.

"But with only a few tables and my preference for writers, I

> *One night Truman Capote came to the entrance and Don said, "I'm not letting fags in here" and turned him away. . . . I bought off Don's share and we parted company.*

Writers Irwin Shaw and George Plimpton

couldn't accommodate all the people who wanted to reserve, and that's how I got the reputation for being so exclusive. After I enlarged the restaurant and put in more tables, I still had to keep a row of tables for my regulars, the writers who used to stay late, play backgammon and poker, and make a second home out of it."

"When Elaine's opened," George Plimpton says, "Nelson Aldrich and Fred Seidel, who were on *The Paris Review* with me, started hanging out there. It seemed very Parisian at the time. People would play cards and backgammon at the tables, and there was a dartboard. The arts crowd had just started drifting in. But it was my feeling that Elaine charged too much, and one night, when I was served an artichoke the size of a walnut that cost five dollars, I went up to her and said, 'Elaine, at "21" they charge the same and their artichokes are the size of a melon.' She screamed out at the top of her voice, 'Take the artichoke off the gentleman's check!' I was so humiliated that I couldn't go in for six months."

"Elaine protected her writers like a lioness protects her cubs," Lewis Lapham, the editor of *Harper's*, says. "I had dinner with a date there one evening when Jack Richardson started up a poker game at a back table. It was a good game in which considerable money was changing hands. My date was a high-spirited young woman who, around two, three in the morning, began to suggest and then, later on, *demand* that I take her home, but not getting any results she began to get vociferous to the point of disturbing the game, and with a crescendo of emotion she picked up her handbag and started beating me over the head with it. Whereupon Elaine immediately materialized, grabbed my irate date, and, together with Donald Ward, ran her down the length of the restaurant and out into the street where Elaine put her in a cab. Then Elaine went into the kitchen and made scrambled eggs for all us poker players."

Michael Caine has also experienced Elaine's omnipotent protection. "One night I was at the table she always reserves for me, sitting alone, waiting for my wife, when a rather tipsy woman came over, plopped herself down next to me, and proceeded to have a chat, but she didn't get very far before Elaine was hovering over her, telling her in no uncertain terms to get back to her own table. The woman looked at Elaine defiantly and said, 'No. I'm going to visit with Michael Caine.' It was then I discovered that no one says no to Elaine when she is protecting one of her beleaguered, for she took the woman by the arm and marched her back to her own table to join her husband. The husband was outraged by Elaine's action, and he stood up and called her a few ungentlemanly names, whereupon Elaine hauled off and punched him forcefully in the nose, knocking him back on his seat—that was the end of that."

I discovered that no one says no to Elaine when she is protecting one of her beleaguered, for she took the woman by the arm and marched her back to her own table to join her husband.

Gay Talese and I were having dinner there one night when we also benefited from Elaine's belligerent protection. An attractive young woman I had never seen before, who had been at the bar, came to our table, sat down next to me, and while chatting with us cheerfully, started eating my lasagna. I assumed she was a friend of Talese's; Talese assumed she was a friend of mine. But she made the fatal mistake of picking up a piece of bread and starting to butter it. At that moment, Elaine was at the bar, totaling up checks but out of the corner of her eye she noticed the butter going on the bread. She marched over to our table and ordered the woman back to the bar. But a few minutes later the woman returned and this time sat down beside Talese and started to eat his lasagna. Elaine stormed over and threw the woman out. In the process she picked up the bread basket and bellowed to the waiter, "Frank, take this away. It's contaminated. Bring some new bread, but leave the lasagna. When a man lets a broad take control of his fork, he suffers the consequences."

In the beginning, when it was touch-and-go whether Elaine's would make it, Elaine, nevertheless, would run a tab for any writer who was temporarily out of funds, even when "temporarily" meant an indeterminate number of years. Larry L. King recalls that "while *The Best Little Whorehouse in Texas* was playing its showcase run at the Actors Studio—and months before I would earn a nickel off it—a dozen Washington politicians came to see it and joined me later at Elaine's. After eating and drinking as if enjoying one last fling before going off to starve, they marched out leaving a bill big enough for them to have voted on and not one thin dime toward appropriations. Elaine, as she had done so many times, told me to pay when I could, and never hectored me to collect. It was good for my ego—if not my solvency—to know that I could always go to Elaine's and spend like a rich Arab even though my telephone had been cut off.

"I liked being able to swagger into Elaine's—wearing ragged blue jeans and a dirty shirt—to plop down at a reserved 'family' table while big butter-and-egg men from Chicago glared or Wall Street finks in their finery shuffled in embarrassment in the standee crush, unable even to secure accommodations in the back room.

"From time to time I've heard people scoff, 'Elaine's is disgusting. A bunch of snooty, social-climbing semicelebrities known

Michael Caine
always checks in
at Elaine's on
his first day in
New York

only to themselves, parading and preening themselves.' Well, hell, everybody needs a stage and room enough to caper. And those critics, it always turned out, couldn't get a table.

"I've had many wonderful times at Elaine's, and I don't suppose it's cost me over two hundred and fifty thousand dollars. I just wish I recalled more of the details."

I n the years before he wrote Forrest Gump, *Winston Groom* also remembers how Elaine supported writers, including himself: "Elaine's was already an institution when I first started going there in the mid-seventies. In those days it was the custom among some of us to keep a running tab. We were never sent a monthly bill or anything like that, we just knew someday we'd have to pay up. At one point my tab was more than seven thousand dollars, accumulated over several years, and Elaine had never said a word. She understood the situation with writers vis-à-vis paydays, and without her I might have starved. Eventually I wrote her a check for the seven thousand; no interest was ever asked. 'Thank you,' was all she said."

There was a newspaper strike two weeks before Christmas in 1962," the author Pete Hamill recalls, "and it would last for four months. None of us had any money. I was a young reporter, married, with a three-month-old baby girl, and started scrambling to find ways to get a paycheck. There was almost no money in our bank account. When the strike was called on December eighth, I was taking home a hundred and nine dollars a week from the *New York Post*. I wasn't alone. There were seven dailies then and thousands of other busted-out journalists were on the street, including some with far greater names than mine, with infinitely more developed talents.

"We made the rounds of the newspaper saloons, hoping some-one would know about a payday. One friend wrote pieces for the *Police Gazette*, for an astonishing fifty dollars each. Another wrote jacket copy for books he hadn't read. A few signed on as flacks for politicians, never to return to our imperfect trade. At some point during that dreadful winter, a few of us heard about this new joint on Eighty-eighth Street and Second Avenue. The owner was help-ing to feed the newspaper refugees.

"That's how I met Elaine Kaufman. In those days, Eighty-

*T*his all happened thirteen years ago. Got a call at work from a journalist snowbound up in Vermont, unable to do research for an article on Elaine's that was due shortly. Could I give background stuff over the phone? Said I didn't know much: Elaine used to have a place downtown, I first went there with Frank Conroy, seemed like a friendly neighborhood bar, et cetera. Journalist said this was all boring and unusable. Didn't anything *interesting* ever happen there?

Only trying to be helpful. Interesting, I thought, what would have been interesting? Picasso coming in and sketching us all? That would have been nice. Rejected this fantasy in favor of one that would have had special meaning for me.

Well, I said, you know that little out-of-tune piano Elaine keeps in the back room? One night the great singer Dietrich Fischer-Dieskau and Leonard Bernstein came in, and for an hour Fischer-Dieskau sang Rodgers and Hart songs and Bernstein played. You don't really know those songs until you hear the world's greatest lieder singer do them.

Never thought that editors, fact checkers, and so forth would let this transparent absurdity get by. But there it was in print a couple months later. One of the legendary "great moments" at Elaine's. A few years later, *Esquire* did an article on the restaurant and there it was again: Fischer-Dieskau, Bernstein, Rodgers and Hart. Obviously the writer had done research, found the story in print, therefore it must be true. Now that it has appeared in two respectable magazines, it's documented history. I'm sorry it never happened—I would have enjoyed it immensely.

—ROBERT BROWN, editor

eighth Street was far beyond the borders of our social world. Occasionally there'd be a good murder that drew us as reporters. Sometimes there'd be labor troubles at the nearby brewery. But for most of us, the newspaper saloons were down beside the *Journal-American* on South Street or the *Post* on West Street, with important outposts in the Village. The farthest north we ever traveled was to Bleeck's, the *Herald-Tribune* bar on Fortieth Street. Second Avenue and Eighty-eighth Street was as remote as Kennebunkport.

"Someone I can no longer remember told us about this new place uptown, and on the rounds, looking for someone who might hire us, we found our way to what became one of New York's great good places. Elaine didn't care that we'd never been there before; she was delighted to see us. And if we had a bowl of pasta, and if she knew we were newspapermen, she'd tear up the check. That was the beginning. Most of us never forgot her for that, and later, when the strike was over, and we started earning money again, we went back.

"We've been going back ever since, in good times and bad, to share the pleasure of her company. Each time we walk in the door, we carry with us a thousand nights of laughter, argument, lies, dispute, over which she served as a kind of conductor. Elaine was full of smart-ass remarks, the old New Yorker's contempt for bullshit, and a high regard for the endless repetitions of human folly. She hasn't changed. In her theology, all sins can be forgiven, except cruelty. She loved lonely souls, or people who stayed up all night playing cards and drinking cognac. When marriages collapsed, including mine, she turned the joint into a living room, helping the melancholy casualties get through the night. Her joint served as the home place for all those who did not want to go home.

"Today, there are ghosts in the place, of course, proof that all of us are mortal. The presence of ghosts is what we call memory. But on any given night, the joint is packed and noisy and shimmers with the energy that Elaine brought to it all those years ago. I see the faces of young people, trying on their acts, lying and disputing and laughing, and their presence warms my heart. Some of them are younger than I was when I first walked in the door. I hope they have as many laughs as I did, and that when they need it, at three o'clock on some rainy morning, they'll also have Elaine there to offer her rough brand of consolation."

I *remember sitting in Elaine's one* night, and there was Valerie Perrine. All the famous people that go in and out of there, and I was sitting next to Honey Bruce. I leaned over and said, "I hope you don't take this the wrong way, but I never wanted to make love to a woman more than I wanted to make love to Honey Bruce." She just smiled and said, "Thank you."

—ALEC BALDWIN, actor

" I was sitting with Tennessee Williams, who was very depressed. We talked for a while and then he picked up a menu and wrote across the top, in Welsh: 'I have lost my way.' He signed it as the Welsh do: 'Tennessee, the Plays.' It was the last time I saw him. **"**

—ELAINE

Everyone Comes to Elaine's

7

From her perch in the restaurant, Elaine unobtrusively monitors all the arrivals and departures

PHOTOGRAPH BY SALLY DAVIES

In the beginning, Elaine barely tolerated women diners, even when they were in the company of her favorite writers. "Our mother didn't have much use for women," her sister, Edith, says, "much preferred male customers, and I guess Elaine inherited that from her."

George Plimpton, who had the wedding reception for his first marriage at Elaine's, and a wedding party with his current wife there, nevertheless acknowledges that women are not favored by Elaine. "Elaine's is like a cocktail party with good atmosphere given by a very good hostess. You never know whom you're going to see except you know you'll see a lot of beautiful girls. There's an electric quality about it. Elaine is tremendously faithful to those she likes. She likes men more than women. She's a little suspicious of women. But she never fawns over you like the maitres d'hôtel in some restaurants. She's also very tough. If people don't behave the way she thinks they should, she'll throw them out. She has the fastest knee in town and she knows where to put it."

"I like women to be straight with me," Elaine says. "Don't play with me, don't make games up, or patronize me. And a lot of women do that. And so the women I get along with best are women who are straight and upfront. I was hostile toward women until I started seeing a female analyst. I learned about what I thought by going to her. That was about the highlight of my forty years on the couch."

Nora Ephron says, "Elaine treated writers' wives as if they were temps, and most of them were. Her customers had to have had the highest divorce rate in the country."

"Elaine is very hard on women," Tommy, the bartender, says. "She'll say, 'She's a bimbo, garbage.' But then there are the others. 'That woman is absolutely beautiful, she's charming, la la la.' If

Women were not welcomed at early Elaine's, except as décor. . . . There were a few exceptions, but all in all it was understood . . . the proprietress was not crazy about the sex.

she's a businesswoman, if she's got something on the ball, if she's intelligent, you got a friend for life with Elaine Kaufman. But if you're a fucking bimbo, looking to wiggle your ass into it, she spots you right away, and lets you know how she feels about you."

"Women were not welcomed at early Elaine's, except as décor," Jules Feiffer says. "There were a few exceptions, but all in all it was understood that the proprietress was not crazy about the sex. Women would cry out in terror when they were told you had made reservations. It was a test of love. If a wife or date still spoke to you after a long evening in which you were celebrated and she

Helen Mirren

PHOTOGRAPH BY JESSICA BURSTEIN

was ignored, few ways remained to damage the relationship."

Bruce Jay Friedman's first wife, Ginger, blames Elaine for driving the last nail into the coffin of her marriage to Bruce. "She said something awful, unrepeatable to me, and Bruce defended her. That was the final nick in the marriage. Elaine is funny, smart, and terrific for men who were never toilet trained properly. And she's no sexual threat. They couldn't handle a sexual woman."

Bruce Jay Friedman's first wife, Ginger, blames Elaine for driving the last nail into the coffin of her marriage to Bruce.

Margaret Croydon, a freelance writer who had the audacity to question a bill she received, says, "What goes on with women has nothing to do with real life. You're like a hunk of furniture. You don't exist. Just some dame a guy brought in."

"I always thought Elaine had her favorites," the writer Barbara Goldsmith says. "I was not one of them. I always thought her favorites were men. One night I was with James Brady, and I asked the waiter to bring us some bread. 'Let Jim speak for himself,' Elaine snapped. Another night I was there with my husband and I asked the waiter to remove the bread. 'Let Frank speak for himself,' Elaine snarled. Then there came a time I was eating dinner when I suddenly felt quite ill. I said I wanted to go home, but someone at the table insisted that all I needed was a stomach settler. 'Bring her a Fernet-Branca,' he told the waiter. Suddenly Elaine was at my side. Her voice boomed out. 'Let Barbara speak for herself.' Then she hugged me."

Gay Talese had a rather peculiar experience that emanated from a woman who had been put on restraints by Elaine. "Elaine Kaufman has long been rather frosty toward women," Gay says, "who venture in without dates or dinner reservations, women who will try to nurse a single drink for an entire hour while seated at one of the bar stools across the aisle from the row of choice tables that

Ms. Kaufman reserves for her favorite male regulars—a group that she occasionally joins for dinner or dessert, and among whom she is everyone's confidante and self-appointed guardian against potential temptresses who might be unmindful of the fact that in *this* room she alone is the principal female attraction.

"I have patronized Elaine's with such regularity for so long that I rarely hear or observe anything new. But on this particular night, while dining at a front table with my wife and a few writer friends, and after excusing myself to venture back to the men's room, I noticed two young women dining together at a corner table in the rear across from where Woody Allen was seated with two of his friends who were familiar to me. One was a banker, who I believe was a sometime investor in Mr. Allen's films, and the other individual, an attractive brunette who resided with the banker, had served as a producer for a few of Allen's films. Woody Allen and his two companions were seated very close together, eating and talking with their head and eyes lowered, indicating that they wished to avoid social contact with the rest of the room while at the same time positioning themselves at the far end of their table in a way that allowed their faces to be visible to nearly all the other diners gathered in the very crowded dining room.

"The two young women across the aisle from Allen's table were taking turns staring at him, waiting in vain for him to look up from his salad and make eye contact; but he ignored them completely. As I passed Allen's table, and made a right turn toward the men's room, I noticed that one of the young women was now watching me. She was a blonde with a round face and wore aviator glasses. I am fairly certain that I had never seen her before.

"Moments later, as I was standing at the urinal, I heard the door open behind me. As I finished and was about to zip up my fly, I turned to see the woman with the aviator glasses standing behind me, leaning against the sink to get a closer view.

"'I just wanted to watch,' she explained matter-of-factly."

I'm the Elaine who does not allow burgers on the premises and they should go somewhere that does and take that fucking cheeseburger with them.

Elaine admits she does have a prejudice but it's largely against "the men who keep the company of those little girls all the time. Sometimes you see this incredible intellect sitting there and trying to talk to them, these little girls who in the original teaching would have been taught to be seen and not heard. That rule has passed out of the book completely. I mean, they know everything. Years ago, it used to be more sophisticated. Then, at least, they would lay back a little. The seduction was a matter of finding something more than was there. These girls, they regurgitate all they know in about twenty minutes and then smear it around for the rest of the time. It's very funny. That's the reason I understand why so many of the men meet in the restaurant and sit around and talk with one another, because sometimes they just can't deal with the kind of conversation they have to put up with. I mean, I truly understand it, because once in a while some girl will throw one in and everybody will just look in disbelief."

And then there are incidents that involve women but are not specifically aimed at their gender. The Molly Ringwald affair, for instance. Elaine came into the place one evening and stopped dead in her tracks at the sight of a cheeseburger on one of her tables, specifically on the table occupied by Molly Ringwald, who was hosting a party of six, including her mother. "A cheeseburger. A fucking cheeseburger!" exclaims Elaine. "I call over my head guy, Gianni,

PHOTOGRAPH BY JESSICA BURSTEIN

'What the hell is that?' 'What is what?' 'What the hell is that god-damned cheeseburger doing on my table?' 'It's Molly Ringwald's mother's,' he says. 'She wanted a cheeseburger—they got it from the deli across the street.' Whereupon I say, politely: 'Remove that god-damned cheeseburger from my table.' One word leads to another, the mother's saying she's never been so insulted, and says, 'Who do you think you are?' And I tell 'em who I am—I'm the Elaine who does not allow burgers on the premises and they should go somewhere that does and take that fucking cheeseburger with them. . . . Well, okay, I guess I was a bit harsh—but you got to maintain your standards."

Michelle Phillips with son-in-law Billy Baldwin celebrating the birth of her grandchild

"I have fallen in love with dozens of beautiful women in Elaine's," Larry L. King says, "and directly approached them to confess it. Most of them wouldn't give me the time of day. A few unfortunately did. I shall never forget the night I approached Lauren Hutton at nine-thirty-six P.M. and she left before it got to be nine-thirty-seven. Elaine fussed at me about that one.

"One night, a tall, lovely, dark-haired actress—quite well known—marched up to my table and berated me in mule skinner's language for not having called in a week. She ordered me home with her. This was quite startling, since I had never met the lady and suffered the complication of being in the presence of my then wife. It took Elaine some time to persuade the tipsy actress—and my wife—that she had the wrong fellow.

"Once, I was hiding from Tom Guinzburg, of Viking Press, whom I owed a hundred and forty thousand dollars in lieu of two long-overdue books. He spotted me anyway and invited me and my date, Kathy, to his table. We dined with Tom and his wife, Rusty; after an initial nervousness, things went smashingly well until the check came. While Tom and I struggled over it, Kathy sang out, 'What the hell, Larry, let him pay! What's another hundred bucks on top of what you owe him now?'"

It should be noted, however, that Elaine has always had a high regard for women of signal accomplishments, women like the distinguished artist Helen Frankenthaler (who early on became a regular when she lived nearby in a town house on Ninety-fourth Street with her then husband, Robert Motherwell), Nora Ephron, Lauren Bacall, Helen Gurley Brown, always accompanied by David, her movie producer husband, Michele Lee, Joan Rivers, Susan Sontag, Betty Comden, Mary Higgins Clark, Barbara Goldsmith, Martha Stewart, Wendy Wasserstein, Phyllis Newman, Lillian Hellman, Mary McCarthy (but never at the same time), Christie Whitman, Sue Mengers, Iman, and Dr. Ruth Westheimer to name but a few.

W"hen I was a student in Paris," says Dr. Ruth, "my friends and I would go to a café and spend hours discussing world politics and our future plans, but we were so impoverished that we often had to share a cup of coffee in order to be able to claim table rights. Having grown up with this European tradition, what the Viennese call *Stammtisch*, I missed it when I first came to New York. Of course I could have gone to a corner bar to talk about the Yankees, except that I don't really drink and know nothing about baseball. The only place in New York, or, in fact, the country, that fills that void for me is Elaine's.

"First of all, there's always somebody there to talk to. I love joining a big group, such as the table that my friend Josh Gaspero often hosts. And I delight in the surprise that comes from seeing familiar faces, either from other nights at Elaine's or from other venues, like the stage and screen, or other noted Europeans who have found their way there. But I've also just dropped in when I didn't know a soul. Elaine would always put me at just the right table, such as the time she sat me with an Israeli publisher, not knowing that he'd published one of my books! Her skills as a matchmaker, at least when pairing people for an evening, are unmatched anywhere.

Elaine would always put me at just the right table. . . . Her skills as a matchmaker, at least when pairing people for an evening, are unmatched anywhere.

PHOTOGRAPH BY JESSICA BURSTEIN

Michele Lee   "Another quality about Elaine and her establishment is that it's gemütlich, or as they say on the other side of the Rhine, cozy. The waiters know that I like herbal tea and also that I like having the Dover sole three nights in a row. Elaine's is my home away from home where I can literally kick my shoes off.

"But the best quality about Elaine's is that nobody talks about the weather. The discussions at Elaine's are literary, intelligent, challenging, outrageous, bawdy, and quite likely to spread across table boundaries, but they're never banal. You can be as loud and boisterous as you want as long as you're not boring. It's an atmosphere that I cherish, and I feel privileged that I am able to enter Elaine's magic kingdom whenever the need arises."

When my husband and I were living on the West Coast," the actress Michele Lee says, "Elaine's was a regular visit whenever we came to New York. Recently we separated, however, and I moved East, but being alone for the first time in years, and certainly not yet interested in going out on 'dates,' I found myself rather isolated. But not for long. Elaine made it clear that I was to call her whenever an empty evening loomed large, and she would tell me who was in the restaurant I might like to join. She would arrange it. Or if there was no one appropriate, she herself would have dinner with me. Elaine is instinctual. She has a bag full of remedies, in deeds and words."

The bestselling novelist Mary Higgins Clark says, "Elaine's is special. You step inside and you will inevitably see someone you haven't seen in ten years or had lunch with yesterday. No matter how busy you've been, how tired you are, you perk up. My daughter Carol and I have celebrated some of our book parties at Elaine's and have wrapped up other very large events by taking over the right-hand room with fifty or sixty or seventy of our friends. Elaine's is fun. Elaine's is unique. And, of course, it exists because it is reigned over by the queen of the in spots, Elaine herself!"

Father Pete   "My husband, Edgar, and I spent many happy nights in Elaine's," says comedienne Joan Rivers. "When we were living in California, it was our first destination when we came to New York because we could immediately meet friends, see people, and let everyone know we were back in town. After Edgar committed suicide, I immediately packed up and moved to New York.

"Now living in New York, the only times I went out were to go with close friends up to Elaine's for dinner, just to get out of the house, and feel I was in warm and comfortable surroundings. It took me a long time to deal with Edgar's death.

"Whenever I came in, Elaine always put me at a table against the wall in the back where I could only be partially seen. It was a very secure place. I would go there at least four nights a week with different friends and just sit and talk. And even though Elaine was usually strict about sitting at a table and not eating, nothing was said when I would just order a drink and no food.

"This went on for weeks, and weeks turned into months, and nothing was ever said like 'Joan Rivers is sitting there and eating nothing on a Saturday night at a table that should hold six and turn over three times.' It wasn't until one Saturday that I looked up and saw the huge crowd in the front and people waiting for tables that I realized how dear and sweet Elaine was. She never ever asked me to move, or asked me to get up, or even asked if I wanted to order. It was finally my decision one night, a Tuesday, when I said, 'Elaine, give me a smaller table—I'm ordering pasta.' She just laughed."

Elaine has always been very compassionate about the tribulations of her family of regulars. Father Pete Colapietro, who has been a regular at Elaine's for over thirty years and occupies a special niche, says that she has helped out his parish in many ways "with her unique form of fund-raising, very similar to the Cardinal Spellman method: You find out who's got the money and then you ask them for it. One night she greeted a couple of guys who were cosmetic executives and had just come in after some benefit—Broadway Cares, I believe. She says, 'You guys just came from a benefit?' They reply, 'Yeah.' Elaine asks, 'You gave them a donation? Listen, we got Father Pete right over here. He's got a church down the block. The place needs a paint job plus the roof leaks, so why don't you guys do something?' She raised ten thousand dollars for us right then and there that night.

"I had an unbelievably horrifying experience about fifteen years ago," Father Pete recalls. "Six of us were out deep-sea fishing, about twenty-five or thirty miles out on the ocean off Hampton Bays, Long Island, when one of our crew, a young man, twenty-one years old, Lawrence Lenihan, fell overboard. A great kid, a senior at Villanova University. We had just finished fishing for the day and were motoring back to the dock. The sea was pretty rough and Larry fell off the stern. Though we searched and searched for hours, we didn't find him. His body was never recovered.

"I was in shock for over a week. Mind you, as a priest I have been with many people in their last moments on this earth, but this was different. Couldn't drive the car, couldn't do anything. I was numb. I finally managed to get myself together for the drive home to New York City. And where did I head? Where could I find people I knew, friends, when it's late at night? I headed to Elaine's, sat down at a table right next to her. I was wearing a T-shirt and shorts, having just come from Long Island. Elaine knew what had happened and she asked, 'How are ya? How ya feeling?' People always ask, 'How are ya? How ya feeling?' but the way she said it was something else. I tried to explain to her what was going on in my mind at that point in time but she just grabbed me and gave me this BIG HUGE HUG, held me to her more than ample bosom as I sat there and wept. She held on to me until I was finished weeping. She made me feel the best I had in over a week. I guess I got it all out and she was the catalyst. She has the reputation of being

Gwyneth Paltrow

PHOTOGRAPH BY JESSICA BURSTEIN

tough as nails but that night she became my 'magnolia of steel.' That night, I will never, ever forget. She showed a side not too many get to see."

Television's *Tom Fontana, writer and producer of Homicide: Life on the Street* and the HBO hit series *Oz*, says, "My single happiest and saddest moment at Elaine's was just before Noel Behn died. Noel, who had written *The Kremlin Letter* among many other books, was one of Elaine's earliest and most constant and devoted attendees—more friend than customer although that he was—four times a week on average. He'd been having trouble getting around, was in and out of the hospital, and was due to go in again. His close friends knew, but never said, that this time would be the last time.

"The night before, I asked Noel where he wanted to go. Big surprise—Elaine's. I called Elaine at home to tell her that we'd be there, but early, since Noel was now tiring easily. Well, Elaine, whom I don't think ever gets up much before seven P.M. did something extraordinary. She showed up for the early dinner. And as the three of us sat there eating, I couldn't help but think about all the history that had passed between the two of them, all the famous people they'd known, all the laughs and heartbreaks they'd shared. I felt honored to listen in on this last conversation between two old friends. I was too young to go with Noel the first night he had dined at Elaine's, but I will treasure forever being there that last time. The memory makes me smile even now.

"After Noel's memorial service, a dinner was held in his honor at Elaine's. He would've loved it!"

Elaine has been an inspiration for many of her neophytes. Bobby Zarem now heads one of the most successful public relations firms in New York, specializing in Hollywood movies and actors, but, he says, "when I worked for the Rogers and Cowan public relations company, I wanted to go out on my own, but I was fearful that I couldn't make a go of it. As a matter of fact, I had already established my credibility—only I didn't know it.

"Elaine urged me to take the step, and to prove her confidence in me she offered to finance me but I didn't want to lose her money—so unconfident was I! Then a group of Wall Street financiers offered to finance me and because I didn't mind losing the money of rich strangers, I tentatively accepted their help. When Elaine found out she yelled at me because I wasn't going to let her, as a friend, help me out, but that I'd let strangers do so. For the first

---

When Mick Jagger is in New York he comes in a lot. He's a very funny guy. Very complicated. He came in a few times with this very nice girl, a Moroccan or something like that, who was trying to make it as an actress. She came in with him one night for supper and she said excitedly, "Elaine, Elaine, I finally got a part." And I said, That's great, sweetheart, I mean, you work so hard. Good for you. She said, "Yeah, I got the lead in this film, and I'm finally going to get a real chance." That's as much as Mick could take. He put his hand on my arm and said, "Hey, Elaine, I'm going to do a movie, too." And I said, Oh, Mick, that's wonderful.

—ELAINE

time, thanks to Elaine, I realized that I had the right stuff to make it on my own. As a result, I took no one's money and started from scratch—it was Elaine who gave me the confidence to believe in myself and take that risk of going out on my own."

So, do you know Sydney Pollack and Bob Redford? I mumbled of course I knew who they were but didn't know them. She grabbed me, and said, "Hey, guys, you need to know this kid. Buy him a drink." And they did.

Morgan Entrekin, *the president and publisher of* Grove Atlantic Press, had a similar experience: "In the fall of 1977 when I moved to New York as a young man starting out in publishing, I was taken to Elaine's for the first time by my friend Helen Bransford, who was from my hometown of Nashville. She invited me to dinner at a table that included Carl Bernstein, P. J. O'Rourke, and George Plimpton. Somehow Elaine took a liking to this young editor and I could always get a table for a date or a young writer I was trying to sign up. Elaine often went out of her way to help me out. I remember one night when I had arrived early and was waiting for my friends, Elaine, at her usual perch at the end of the bar, said to me, 'So, do you know Sydney Pollack and Bob Redford?' I mumbled of course I knew who they were but didn't know them. She grabbed me, took me over to the table where they were sitting, and said, 'Hey, guys, you need to know this kid. Buy him a drink.' And they did.

"As a young editor, hanging out at Elaine's with writers was a much more productive way for me to find books to publish than going to lunch with agents. And a hell of a lot more fun. One night I was at dinner with Terry McDonell and P. J. O'Rourke. P.J. had recently left *National Lampoon* and started freelancing. He had written a piece for Terry on drug etiquette with which he proceeded to entertain the table. When I stopped laughing, I turned to P.J. and said, 'Why don't you turn that into a book for me?' Thus was born P.J.'s first book, *Modern Manners: An Etiquette Book for Rude People.* That was the first of ten books that P.J. would write—all of which I published. I have signed up other authors at Elaine's, including George Plimpton and William Hamilton. We did eventually come up with a rule that any deal done after midnight had to be confirmed by both sides the next day.

"Eventually, with a certain amount of trepidation, I left Simon and Schuster to try and start my own publishing venture. I was taking a big risk and a lot of people were skeptical that I could make it work. The first time I was in Elaine's after going out on my own, Elaine took me into the side room, sat me down, and offered to invest in my company. I was speechless. I had already raised all the money I needed but I will never forget that offer. And the fact that Elaine believed that I could pull it off was worth more than money to me."

The actor John Henry Kurtz
literary agent Bob Datilla, producer Dick Wolf, and actor Peter McCabe, and I were having dinner when Peter noticed a model who had been in a *Miami Vice* episode he'd written. Peter—as usual, impeccably dressed, not a wrinkle, as if he wore his suit jacket with the hanger still in it—went up to her, introduced himself, and, after a half an hour of chit-chat, left with her.

The following week, Peter noticed another model—beautiful but so thin she looked constructed of Tinkertoys—who'd been in the same episode. Again, he went up to her, introduced himself, and left with her.

Dick, John Henry, and I decided Peter was having too much fun.

The following week, John Henry called Peter to warn him that Dick and I had arranged a practical joke: We'd hired a transvestite to pick up Peter.

So that Thursday night, when a beautiful—but somewhat big-boned—woman at the bar gave Peter the eye, Peter didn't respond. The woman sauntered over to our table, sat next to Peter, and started to flirt.

Nervously, Peter checked for telltale signs of an Adam's apple, studied the size of her hands, and noticed how she crossed her legs as the woman caressed Peter's hair and whispered in his ear.

When she went to the ladies' room, Peter said, "Guys, it's not going to work. John Henry warned me."

But the warning was a setup.

We explained to Peter that his date was, in fact, not a transvestite, but an actress we'd hired to pretend to be one. A little innocent fun. We thought.

When the actress came back from the ladies' room, Peter took her in his arms and gave her a kiss.

Within twenty minutes, Peter and the actress were gone. And Elaine handed around to John Henry, Dick, and me notes Peter had left for us, saying "You hired her. I'm going home with her."

However . . . in the taxi, on the way to Peter's apartment, the actress told Peter the reason she had been chosen to pretend to be a transvestite was that she was, in fact, a transsexual.

The actress, who, in fact, was not a transsexual—that was sting two—claimed Peter said, "I don't care what you are. You're gorgeous."

Peter claimed he knew the actress was not a transsexual and was just calling her—and our—bluff.

In any case, the actress had left her purse at Elaine's, so Peter turned the taxi around, and they both came back and rejoined the table.

—DAVID BLACK, writer and producer

"The first book party was given here in 1967 by Tom Guinzburg of Viking Press for *Stop-Time* by Frank Conroy. We had flamenco dancers. We had the New York Rock and Roll Ensemble led by Michael Kamen, who is now doing film scores. And we had a stripper. China Machado told me, if you hire a stripper, make sure she is very beautiful and very amusing. So this Korean-Italian girl came in wearing a leather motorcycle jacket. I stared at her and thought I'm in trouble. She doesn't look amusing or beautiful. But then the girl went into the ladies' room and got dressed in an Oriental emerald gown and suddenly was magnificent. That was the first of about four hundred book parties that have been given here."

—ELAINE

Everyone Comes to Elaine's

8

A toast by Willie Morris

PHOTOGRAPH BY JESSICA BURSTEIN

The preposterous years of the sixties coincided with the preposterous years of Elaine's. Nightly the saloon was filled with young, festive people in outrageous costumes, feather boas and mismatched military uniforms, circus tights and clown garb, rock stars both compos and noncompos, like Mick Jagger facedown in his spaghetti, the Who and Chubby Checker, LSD and psychedelic posters, as if Elaine's were the branch headquarters for King's Road.

Elaine Stritch, desperately wanting to avoid the boring rigors of an impending season of summer stock, talked Elaine into letting her tend bar.

The actress Elaine Stritch, desperately wanting to avoid the boring rigors of an impending season of summer stock, talked Elaine into letting her tend bar. The incomparable British comedienne Bea Lillie, resplendent with her signature strand of pearls, came to dinner expressly to witness the spectacle of Stritch behind the bar, as did the costume jewelry designer Kenneth Jay Lane, who was under the impression that the restaurant was named after her. Noël Coward also came in to verify with his own eyes that Stritch was a functioning barmaid. Coward had written the musical *Sail Away* for Stritch but he had been unaware of her secondary talent. Coward had also given her a dachshund, which she kept with her behind the bar. There were quitting times, however, when Stritch hurried off into the night and forgot about the dog, and it remained stranded in the restaurant overnight. One busy evening, Elaine recalls, Stritch disappeared momentarily and the next thing Elaine knew, Stritch was feeding the dog a pot roast that she had taken from a downstairs refrigerator.

Nora Ephron, who wrote and directed *Sleepless in Seattle, You've Got Mail,* and other hits, remembers "a lawyer named Jimmy Siff, who got into trouble because of the drug stuff that was going on. He was a great guy. Everyone did some coke in that period, some

Paul Simon, striking a waiter's pose in the Elaine's kitchen

Nora Ephron and
Nick Pileggi

people more than others; it was usually purchased from the dealer that Bruce Jay Friedman wrote about in the great Harry Towns stories. The dealer with the white polar bear rug on the wall. He was almost unreachable, and many nights were spent leaving messages on his machine and waiting for him to call back. Some nights we'd reach him, some nights we wouldn't. Some nights someone would score drugs at Eric's, the bar across the street."

"That was the period," editor Bob Brown says, "when David Halberstam was breaking up with Elzbieta. I was at the table one night when David got mad at Elzbieta because she stole a cherry tomato from his salad. He had a tantrum.

"It was also a time when women had to be very careful about their purses. Thieves would come into the place and walk down the aisle to the back room, spot a purse hanging on the back of a chair, and just lift it off as they walked out."

Nora Ephron remembers *"one night some professional* football players got into a fight about something. People were often drunk, sometimes in fights, and sometimes thrown out by Elaine for something or other. It was sort of like hockey—the possibility of low-key violence was always there, but it rarely happened. Nonetheless it made things a little exciting. My memory is that Lewis Lapham and Willie Morris had some sort of encounter over *Harper's* magazine, and a punch may have been thrown. That was about as violent as it got.

"Whenever anything happened in New York life, at least in the magazine world, you went up to Elaine's that night to see people and talk about it. The day Rupert Murdoch bought *New York* magazine out from under Clay Felker, everyone at the magazine quit and went to Elaine's. The night of the second New York blackout, Carl Bernstein—we were married then—came in from Washington and met me at Elaine's. Everyone sat at tables on the sidewalk that night and ate by candlelight.

"My first real script deal came about because I was at Elaine's when Mark Rosenberg from Warner Bros. came in with Anthea Sylbert."

The writer Tommy Thompson, *who died a few years ago,* remembered, "There was this one night Jason Robards stood up on his chair and announced that I was an unethical liar because I had written an article about him and mentioned in about the forty-eighth paragraph that he took a drink now and then. But then he swayed in midaccusation and fell toward his tumbler, saved from possible hurt by the quick reflexes of Christopher Plummer. Another night, Mia Farrow comes in, she brings in twenty-five peo-

"The most incredible thing that ever happened," Tom Wolfe says, "is that I was there one night and someone listened to what was being said at the table!"

ple a few nights after her divorce from Sinatra, and he comes in too, unannounced. Leopold Stokowski comes in with his sons and is seated by the jukebox and he tells Elaine he is a musician—'I'm supposed to not know that maybe?' answers Elaine—and perhaps he could move from the music. Black limousine rolls up—Lord Snowden emerges. Jackie Kennedy is in. Lynda Bird is in with George Hamilton, and Secret Service men demand an adjoining free table to protect them. 'What's to protect?' proclaims Elaine. 'What am I supposed to do for a living? Nobody's gonna bother 'em here, nobody even cares.' The protectors are banished to the jukebox. Angela Lansbury and Natalie Wood and Terence Stamp, who pays in pounds, they all come in, the hyphenated names, the senatorial names, the princely names."

*T*he writers' table is packed: playwright Arthur Kopit, Styron, Bruce Jay Friedman, Ephron, Hotchner, Jack Gelber, Halberstam, Nicholas Pileggi, Peter Maas, and so on, a virtual roll call of the Authors Guild. "The most incredible thing that ever happened," Tom Wolfe says, "is that I was there one night and someone listened to what was being said at the table! I don't remember what it was. I wasn't listening myself. I was too busy looking at the people at the next table."

Jerry Orbach, star of *Law & Order*, was at the table one night when Jack Richardson said the evening was full of *joie de mort* after a bag lady walked through to use the john, and minutes later, when a scabbed and bloody wino came in, the great sax jazz musician Paul Desmond said to him, "She just left!"

"That was the night," Orbach says, "when the crossword puz-

zle maven Mary Ann Madden started a contest to make a Polish joke with the punch line 'Downtown Warsaw.' Mine was 'Where does the number seventeen bus to Krakow wind up?'"

With the sixties hubbub swirling around her, Elaine herself occasionally joined the dance. Liz Smith says, "On one occasion I brought my handsome younger brother, Bobby, to Elaine's. He was visiting from Texas, a hearty fellow who has a great affection for alcoholic beverages. Well, sir, he took one look at Elaine and fell in love, and she responded coyly to his Texas hogwash. Next thing I knew, in the midst of all the hoot and holler, they had disappeared to spend the night together. He hasn't come up to visit since then but he often asks about her and speaks glowingly of their night."

Writer Jack Richardson and The Who's Pete Townsend

The unprincipled, extroverted gossip columnist of *London's Daily Mail*, Nigel Dempster, a self-avowed "fortune hunter, drunk, gambler, and lecher," is at a table with Jim Brady, then of the *National Star*, and other professional gossips. At an adjoining table is the veteran actor Kevin McCarthy, Betty Comden, Adolph Green, and George Plimpton. Dempster offers George personal amnesty from getting clobbered in the guest column he is writing for *New York* magazine in exchange for literary dirt that George might dish him, but George says he doesn't bargain with news-hounds, whereupon Dempster drops to the floor on all fours and starts to bark menacingly at Plimpton, then lunges at him, biting him ferociously in the right calf, while shouting, "He's a paper lion! He's a paper lion!" George retreats fearfully and goes to get his leg bandaged.

After Dempster returns to his table, one of the men asks him if he always behaves so badly. "At this moment in history," retorts Dempster proudly, "how else is one expected to behave but *monstrously*!"

In contrast to the abrasive Dempster, there was a beloved gossip columnist, Neal Travis, who created Page Six of the *New York Post*, who often held court at his favorite Elaine's table, gathering items for his column right up until his death from cancer in 2002.

Carlo, the veteran waiter, says, "Back there, in the sixties, the place was really jumping—lively poker games and very heated darts, big bets on darts, and once in a while big fights, especially over the darts, smashing champagne glasses against the wall and each other, that sort of thing. We were supposed to close down by four A.M. but the losers never wanted to leave. So many times I locked up at seven A.M. It wasn't only the poker and darts players who stayed, but we'd get crowds from Studio Fifty-four every night after two A.M. when it closed. They'd come to Elaine's to eat and keep partying. I don't believe Studio Fifty-four served food because they'd come in hungry as hell. Some big-shot kids—Grace Kelly's children, the Kennedy kids, King Emmanuel's grandson, English kids with titles. The jukebox, which played stuff off the top of the charts, and the cigarette machine really got a workout."

In the summer of 1992, I got a call from P. J. O'Rourke, who was coming to town for one night to meet Jann Wenner and Hunter Thompson. They were flying down to Little Rock, Arkansas, the next day to interview Bill Clinton, the recently selected Democratic nominee for president. P.J. invited me to join them at Elaine's for dinner. As the evening progressed, Hunter started pulling various gadgets out of his pockets—a laser pen, some kind of strange flashlight— stuff he was going to give to Clinton. Finally, he pulled out a Baggie of psilocybin mushrooms, threw it on the table, and said, "Fuck if he didn't inhale—I'm putting these in his eggs tomorrow."

—MORGAN ENTREKIN, publisher

" Nureyev was in here one night when I introduced him to Arnold Schwarzenegger, who right away started in on Nureyev about his upper body, how he could develop his biceps, his pectorals, all that shit. So I pulled Arnie away from the table and we talked about his new book, *Pumping Iron*. He didn't have a foreign publisher so I told him to talk to Sir Gordon White in London—I knew him from the times he came in here. Arnie got hold of him and, sure enough, they made a European book deal. **"**

—ELAINE

Everyone Comes to Elaine's

9

Arnold Schwarzenegger
entering Elaine's

PHOTOGRAPH BY RON GALELLA

Regardless of an ambivalence about the food, certainly no one goes to Elaine's for the gustatory creations or the wine cellar or the floral decorations. The thing people go for is not on the menu. Nevertheless, critiques flourish.

"One night we were all at the big table," Nora Ephron recalls, "and were still on our drinks when Elaine sat down with us and was served the evening special. It was a rock Cornish hen stuffed with wild rice. She decimated it. When she got done, all that was left on her plate was a mass of little toothpick bones that had been absolutely picked clean. We had all watched her suck every morsel off the damn thing, and it looked as if it was a fantastic, if aberrational, episode in the life of her kitchen. So all six of us at the table ordered it. It was inedible."

Without a doubt it is the best veal chop in New York, rosy pale, thick, tender, and succulent.

"It is fashionable to complain about the food," author Jay McInerney has said, "even if, or especially if, you have never eaten there. Food, of course, is not the issue at an institution like this, though in fact it's hard to think of another institution like this—a big tree house on the Upper East Side of Manhattan. Does anybody know what the food was like at the Algonquin in the Round Table days?"

"Well, what about the food?" asks Barbara Kafka, author of a dozen cookbooks. "It isn't fancy, but it is possible to have a really excellent meal if one stays within the strong points of the kitchen. Without a doubt it is the best veal chop in New York, rosy pale, thick, tender, and succulent. The steaks are good, particularly the T-bone, the spinach is impeccably clean—creamed, leaf, or with garlic and oil. A first-rate Caesar salad or roasted peppers with fresh anchovies can start a meal, or try an artichoke with all the work done—the leaves arranged like petals of a flower and the cleaned heart at the center. On the right night of the week there is an ample chicken-vegetable soup with large, tender chunks. There is a good Oreo cheesecake and these are just a few of my favorites.

"There are splendid wines. However," Kafka notes, "it was neither food nor alcohol on its own that brought me to Elaine's all those many years ago. It was Paul Desmond, the great sax player with the wordplay sense of humor and gentle manner. He was one of Elaine's men—mainly writers—who tended to gather at the large round table along the right-hand wall as you entered—the good side. Long before the movie stars, gossip columnists, baseball owners, and football players discovered the place, these writers were the heart of the place. When some of them couldn't afford their bar bills, Elaine, the softy with the demeanor of a tough guy, quietly forgave their bills.

"As a lesser mortal and a female, I was seated at a smaller table, but on that favored side at the right. Mary Ann Madden, creator of fabulous wordplay games for *New York* magazine, sometimes sat with us. Jerry Lieber, both musician and poet of lyrics, was often there; but it wasn't yet a showbiz and star place. I think it changed when Woody Allen took to coming in with a posse to a large round table that he virtually owned, just beyond the doorway toward the kitchen. He was the drinker of fabulous wines."

Cosmopolitan's Helen Gurley Brown says, "You don't go to Elaine's necessarily for the food but how can I say that? I never had a bad meal! Spinach and bacon salad, calamari, clams and linguini, are my special friends. In a funny way, I think you go to Elaine's because it is a *happening*. I don't mean a party is always in progress, though many are, but the restaurant *itself* is a 'personality'—because of its owner and because of its clients you just feel 'action' is indigenous to its being."

"The great thing about Elaine's is the safety," says humorist P. J. O'Rourke. "For instance, I'm safe from the food. Every other place in New York seems to be specializing in some horrible gustatory fad: Tibetan dirt salads or Provençal escargot sorbets. God help us if Manhattan restaurateurs ever discover the anthropophagous entrées of the New Guinea highlands. But Elaine never serves me a fish that isn't dead yet or a Bolivian guinea pig terrine."

Look, this is a late-night saloon and occasionally it's necessary to assert myself when things get a little out of hand.

The legendary comic Don Rickles says that when he was performing at the Copa, Elaine's was always a home way from home. "She always joined our table, recommended items from her menu for us, and then ordered coffee for herself. She must know something.

"I remember one night coming out of Elaine's quite late. A homeless man came up to my wife and me and asked for some money. My classic line is always the same: 'Here's five dollars . . . buy yourself a ranch.' Minutes later, he came running up beside us and said, 'Now I need cattle!' Even the homeless are in the Elaine tradition!"

Back in 1966, when I was appearing in Cactus Flower on Broadway," Lauren Bacall says, "I discovered this informal restaurant, more like a literary saloon than a restaurant, where I could go after the show with cast members or alone and find a welcoming atmosphere and a late-night kitchen that fit perfectly for an actress who had just had her adrenaline flowing onstage. And Elaine was always there to seat me, sit with me, share her wonderful New York wisdom and gossip. On those occasions

PHOTOGRAPH BY JESSICA BURSTEIN

when some besotted fellow from the bar wobbled up to mimic the 'whistle' dialogue I had directed at Bogie, Elaine was instantly there to buffer him and steer him back to the bar. Friendly, wise, protective, she introduced me to people she knew I would like to meet—she is a genius at mixing and matching. When I was married to Jason Robards, Elaine's was his favorite after-theater spa, after McSorley's, that is, which was his absolute favorite, and whenever I was on Broadway, Elaine's was an integral part of my repertoire.

Don Rickles in a rare benevolent moment

When I was in *Applause*, I'd go there with Len Cariou, Penny Fuller, and other cast members because Elaine's, with its theatricality, music, and spontaneity, was like a continuation of being on-stage, a place where you could let down slowly from your performance. And when I was in *Woman of the Year*, Elaine's was again a necessary after-performance hangout. Elaine is the most intuitive person I know. She knows me, knows where I come from. All that, and a good bowl of spaghetti Bolognese."

None of Elaine's aficionados is more devoted to her menu than Yankee owner George Steinbrenner. "Elaine is just like a part of my family," he says. "When they're in New York, all my kids, including my grandchildren, insist on eating nowhere else but Elaine's. Recently Stephen Swindal, my grandson, and his entire class from Berkley School went to dinner at Elaine's. She is her own lady and we all love her.

"My devotion to Elaine's is best illustrated by what happened when the Yankees won the famous Subway Series in 2000. All of New York was abuzz and turned on everywhere. The city was on fire with baseball fans all over the streets. I had a lot of guests in from all over the country, and we were all going out to dinner after the game to celebrate. When everyone asked where we should go, I replied that there was only one place and that was to my girl-friend's, Elaine's. I said she'll surely have room for us even if no one else does, because she's family. So all the cars in our group pulled up in front of Elaine's. I said I'm going to the door to get our table. I went up to the door and there was a big burly security cop at the door waving me off, saying sorry, we're full. I said I think she's ex-

PHOTOGRAPH BY JESSICA BURSTEIN

George Steinbrenner regards Elaine's as a home away from home

pecting me. He said, 'Look Mac, I said we're full!' So I turned around and left. I really don't think he knew that we were the Yankees. I was stymied because I could think of no other place in New York that had the right atmosphere in which to celebrate. We sat there at the curb for a while, scratching our heads, but we ended up going back to the hotel where my guests and I were staying, and had a late hamburger in the restaurant. I lost a lot of face with my guests who considered Elaine's the top place in town to celebrate. To have me failing in my guests' eyes on one of the biggest nights of my career was like blowing a save in the last of the ninth."

The composer Cy Coleman says, "When Hotch and I work together on one of our collaborative efforts, we ease the tension of staring at each other when we're temporarily out of ideas by going to Elaine's where, no matter how late it is, the kitchen is in full swing and the saloon is lively. It also helps when you're going through the rigors of rehearsal for a new musical. Larry Gelbart, the writer, Michael Blakemore, the director, and I would cap off our long stretch of rehearsal for *City of Angels* by going there, and when I was doing *The Will Rogers Follies*, Betty Comden, Adolph Green, and I regularly topped off the strain of previews at Elaine's, as I also did with *The Life*."

Many actors, dancers, directors, composers, playwrights, and musicians were finding refuge in Elaine's preserve. When Peter Falk was performing in *The Prisoner of Second Avenue*, he regularly came to Elaine's after the curtain fell like so many others: Neil Simon, frequently, and Brian Dennehy, Peter O'Toole, Richard Burton, Bernadette Peters, Laurence Olivier, Robert De Niro, Lucille Ball, Warren Beatty, Bobby Short, Ingrid Bergman, Shirley MacLaine, Leonard Bernstein, George Balanchine, Edie Falco, Valerie Perrine, Elizabeth Taylor, Judy Garland with Liza, Charles Bronson, Kevin Kline, Alec Baldwin, Isaac Stern, Edward Albee, Dustin Hoffman, Stephen Sondheim, Paul Newman and Joanne Woodward, Al Pacino, Yo-Yo Ma, Clint Eastwood—a roll call of the brightest stars in the American entertainment firmament.

George Steinbrenner started coming here soon after he aquired the Yankees. He's been a staunch friend. I know the family, the children, since they were little kids. He often comes in alone to sit with me and have dinner. People ask me why here, since he could go to any of the upscale eateries in town. I guess it's because I'm no-nonsense, I'm straight, what you see is what you get. He enjoys conversing with someone who doesn't want any favors. And he listens. That's something I'm finicky about—having a conversation with somebody who's not listening, looking around, not really hearing me. There's no exchange going on. When I talk with George there's solid back and forth. He comes in, we can pick up where we left off, even if a couple of months have passed. I'm truly interested in what he does, in what he has to say. There's a side of George that isn't known. The fun side of him. He's an incredible pianist, a knockout. We've had Thanksgiving parties and Christmas parties where George would perform, a smile on his face as bright as the Christmas tree.

—ELAINE

// **Roman Polanski met an attractive girl here one night but didn't seem to like her. I said, 'But she's very clever,' and Roman answered, 'I don't want the competition.'**//

—ELAINE

Everyone Comes to Elaine's

10

Roman Polanski flanked by
movie associates, 1970

By the end of the sixties, the fickle worlds of New York and Hollywood had anointed Elaine's as their capital, thereby seriously breaching the geographical taboo of Eighty-eighth Street, a ceaseless roll call of the rich and illustrious crowding into the unpretentious Second Avenue saloon, which by now had acquired additional space (the grocery next door had gone belly-up and Elaine bought it along with the rest of the building, which included several rent-producing apartments) and increased in size to twenty-three tables that could accommodate anywhere from sixty-five to eighty people, depending on Elaine's skill at mixing and matching, but notwithstanding many "important" diners had to endure waiting time standing at the bar. Elaine had done nothing, however, to enhance the rather dark, drab interior she had inherited, other than proudly to hang the framed jackets of books that her struggling neophyte writers were now producing. Elaine says, "Visually my place may be very ordinary, but emotionally it has a lot. It's very provocative."

Provocative in more ways than one. "Albert Finney came in early one evening in 1982, not many customers yet, when he was rehearsing for the movie *Annie*," Elaine recalls. "He says, 'Elaine, darling, you've got to help me. I've got this big number before the cameras tomorrow—I'm Daddy Warbucks singing and moving all over the place but I'm not ready.'

"'So, what can I do?'

"'Singing's not my long suit and I need to rehearse.'

"'Where?'

"'Here. With you and all your waiters.'

"'Albert, this is a restaurant. We don't rehearse.'

"'If you don't do this for me, you're all poofters.'

Visually my place may be very ordinary, but emotionally it has a lot. It's very provocative.

Elaine introduces
George Segal and
Barbra Streisand

"'We're what?'

"'Poofters.'

"'What kind of a goyisha word is that?'

"'A poofter is what you don't want to be, Elaine.'

"'God forbid.'

"So he takes a recorder from his pocket, turns on the music for 'I Don't Need Anything but You,' and he rehearses, me as little orphan Annie, would you believe? Got all my waiters to dance up and down around the tables with him."

When anyone in here fouls up the etiquette," Elaine says, "I let him know it. Like the night Ben Gazzara was having dinner with Nick Pileggi, Pete Hamill, and the public relations guy John Scanlon. 'Gazzara,' I say, 'what the hell's this tip—ten bucks on a hundred-dollar check. What are you—a ten-percent piker trying to stiff my waiters?'

"'Your waiters!' he says. 'The only time they come near my table is to get the tip.'

"'They know you're a piker!'

"'And what do they bring me? Calf liver from a goddamn steer!'

"'Aha! So now Mr. Piker's a gourmet!'

"'It's gourmand! Yeah—and you wouldn't know Fegato alla Veneziana from third base.'

"'Oh, yeah! I'll tell you what I know—twenty percent of one hundred is twenty. Twenty bucks, Gazzara—the one with Andrew Jackson on it.'

"'Well, I left 'em Alexander Hamilton, which is more than they deserve.'

"So I yell out, 'Okay, give the tenner back to Gazzara—he needs it more than the waiters.'

"'Finito! Finito!' he explodes on his way out. 'I'll never set foot in this clip joint again!'

"When Ben opened on Broadway in Eugene O'Neill's *Hughie*, I gave him a party, and we kissed and made up. From that time on, Ben always leaves twenty percent."

Over the years, Geraldo Rivera has provoked a series of exasperating encounters in the restaurant, each one followed the day after with a bunch of flowers delivered to Elaine accompanied by a note of apology. But the most recent encounter went beyond flowers.

What the hell's this tip—ten bucks on a hundred-dollar check. What are you—a ten-percent piker trying to stiff my waiters?

Geraldo Rivera before he and Elaine lost their sunny rapport

"Geraldo reserves a table for fifteen for dinner," Elaine says. "The big Woody table. It's a full night and I have to turn customers away. In Geraldo comes with his mob and they order drinks—and that's all. Two guys order salads. The other thirteen are white wine and diet Pepsis and sit on them for a couple of hours.

"'So, Geraldo—is this a dinner party or what?'

"'What's it look like?'

"'It looks like everyone's on the fucking Atkins diet.'

"'Elaine, don't start.'

"'Then *you* start—with the menu. You'll see we serve solid food here. For liquids, we have a bar.'

"'Elaine, can we talk?'

"We go into the side room, which happens to be empty.

"'You shouldn't embarrass me in front of my friends,' Geraldo says.

"'Look, Geraldo, when you bring in fifteen people to eat dinner, they have to *eat*!'

"'I give the waiters good tips.'

"'Tips! In case you haven't noticed, I run a business here, which ain't the Ford Foundation.'

"'And in case you haven't noticed, this is a free country where der Führer Elaine Kaufman can't order us to eat her cockamamie food.'

"'Geraldo, you are always trying to get by on the cheap. One diet Pepsi does not equal a veal chop.'

"'Who you calling cheap? I can buy and sell this joint ten times over. Give me the check—we're leaving.'

"I tore up his check in little pieces and threw them at him. 'Good riddance,' I said, 'and don't send me any of your fucking flowers tomorrow.'"

The writer Anthony Haden-Guest says, "*Elaine's strength* is everyone's fear of the irrational mother.

"I always spend the first and last nights in New York in Elaine's," Michael Caine says. "I guess you'd call it the fear factor because her network of information is such that I'm sure if I dared to go to another restaurant, she'd find out about it."

The novelist Winston Groom agrees and when he visits New York from his home in the South, he considers initial attendance at Elaine's a requisite. He also tells a story that illustrates the firm grip that Elaine has on who does what in her preserve. "This happened back in the seventies," Groom says. "Elaine's had become the 'in' place in New York by then because of all the famous writers and, subsequently, movie stars who frequented the place. Somehow this news leaked out to Kansas City, Missouri, and an editor at the newspaper there decided to send a reporter to New York to do a feature on the place and its distinguished guests. This young man arrived at Elaine's at the usual Kansas dinner hour of five-thirty or six P.M., and was astonished to find the place completely empty. At some point Elaine wandered in and the reporter approached her to describe his mission. She liked him, but informed him that his quarry would not even begin showing up until about eight-thirty or nine, then steered him to what we called the 'family table.' This was a place along the famous entrance wall where bachelors, the recently or soon to be divorced, celebrities who had forgotten to make reservations, and other orphans were seated. And she laid down the rules: no photographs and no going up and talking to the other patrons. Sooner or later, she informed the young reporter, some of the writers or movie stars would come and be seated at the 'family table,' and when

Her network of information is such that I'm sure if I dared to go to another restaurant, she'd find out about it.

they did she would introduce him and then he could talk to them and get grist for his story.

Two things happened that night. The first was that it was one of the biggest nights for famous names ever to converge on Elaine's at the same time. Norman Mailer was there and William Styron. Irwin Shaw came in with Rod Steiger, and George Plimpton arrived with his customary entourage. Woody Allen and Diane Keaton seated themselves at his usual table in the back. Pete Hamill showed up, and Joseph Heller, Gay Talese, Dan Jenkins, Lauren Bacall, Kevin McCarthy, and Ryan O'Neal made their entrances. At one point Barbra Streisand swept through the door, wearing some kind of sequined gown that made her look like she had been set on fire.

At one point Barbra Streisand swept through the door, wearing some kind of sequined gown that made her look like she had been set on fire.

"But the second thing was, nobody showed up to sit at the 'family table,' where the reporter from Kansas reposed alone, stewing in his juice. Nine o'clock turned into ten and ten into ten-thirty, and still the 'family table' was empty, save for the reporter, who was now becoming desperate. His head craned from side to side as though he were at a tennis match. From time to time Elaine would abandon her usual place by the cash register and plop down next to him with reassuring words that somebody famous or rich would soon come his way, but this was not to be. The place was abuzz with animated laughter, cigarette and cigar smoke clouded the room, the clink of ice in glasses resounded off the walls, and the reporter knew he was missing his big New York story. Finally, near midnight, he became agitated and almost frantic, and at one point screwed up the courage to ask Elaine if she might just this once bend the rules and let him go over and interview some of the great luminaries who had gathered there that star-studded night.

"Elaine shook her head, no; her rules were not to be bent, and the reporter from Kansas was left only to guess at what wondrously important things the huddled literati were saying to one another at the surrounding tables—so near and yet so far away.

"Finally he turned to Elaine in one last savage act of journalism. 'If you won't let me talk to them,' he said, 'then can't you at least tell me what they are talking about?' Without missing a beat, Elaine replied, 'What are they talking about? Well, they're talking about what *all* writers talk about: baseball, money, and pussy!'

"To this day no one knows for sure whether this useful information ever reached the newspaper subscribers way back in Kansas."

Barry Diller and
Marisa Berenson

PHOTOGRAPH BY JESSICA BURSTEIN

George *Plimpton recounts a similar experience but* with a happier ending.

"Years ago, channel twelve, the Philadelphia public television station, had a fund-raising auction with a vast number of items offered, one of which was called A Night on the Town with George Plimpton. I told the producers down there that they were welcome to offer such a thing, but I doubted it would fetch very much.

"Some weeks later I was telephoned and told that a gentleman named Jerry Spinelli had bid and paid four hundred and some-odd dollars to the television station for the 'Evening.' He and his wife would be coming up to New York.

"I wondered vaguely what to do with them. We have a pool table at home. Perhaps the thing to do was to invite them home for drinks; we'd play some pool and then leisurely we'd eat at some Midtown restaurant—perhaps Gallagher's Steakhouse—so it would be an easy matter to put the Spinellis on a sensible train back to Philadelphia. I didn't know what else to suggest. I had called Spinelli to see if he and his wife would enjoy the theater. Was there anything in particular they would like to see?

"'Oh, no,' he had said in an odd, strangled voice. He seemed very shy.

"'How about pool?' I asked. 'Would you like to shoot a bit of pool?'

"'Pool!'

"A couple of weeks later, the Spinellis turned up at the apartment. They arrived at seven o'clock. 'How about a spot of pool?' I said to Mr. Spinelli. He was a thin, young man with a quick, furtive smile.

"While Mr. Spinelli and I played a somewhat desultory game, my wife took Mrs. Spinelli, whose name was Eileen, to show her the apartment. It was on their tour that my wife discovered the circumstances of the Spinellis' presence. While the Spinellis were looking at some books in the library, she pulled me out into the hall. She whispered hurriedly, 'Jerry Spinelli's a writer.'

"'Oh God.'

"'He's writing a novel.' She went on to say that apparently he worked in the dawn, before he went off to his job, and also when he returned home in the evening. The writing had not been going well. That fateful night, Eileen Spinelli had been watching the channel twelve TV auction—her husband flat out and exhausted in the bedroom—and when the 'Plimpton Evening' was offered, she telephoned in her bid on impulse, feeling that the logjam in her husband's literary career might be broken by having a New York literary 'connection.'

"'Oh Lord!'

"'To pay for this,' my wife said, 'Eileen Spinelli told me she took about everything they had out of savings. Four hundred and twenty-five dollars. She left five dollars in there to keep the account open.'

"'What about the husband when he found out?'

"'He was shocked.'

"I glanced into the library. The Spinellis were leafing through a large book on the coffee table.

"I wondered aloud if we shouldn't somehow pay the couple's debt to channel twelve and make ourselves the donors.

"'We don't live in Philadelphia,' my wife said, practically.

"'Then we'll have to turn this into a literary evening.'

"'They won't enjoy Gallagher's Steakhouse.'

"'No.'

"'We'll have to go to Elaine's.'

"When I told the Spinellis that we were going to Elaine's, Jerry Spinelli brightened visibly. He had heard a lot about it. 'Do you think anybody'll be there?'

When I told the Spinellis that we were going to Elaine's, Jerry Spinelli brightened visibly. He had heard a lot about it. "Do you think anybody'll be there?"

On the way up by taxi, I murmured a prayer that there would be a good literary crowd in Elaine's . . . at the very least the *Saturday Night Live* crowd, who seemed to get twenty of their number around a small table and all talk at the same time; if no luck there, perhaps a couple of *Esquire* editors could be pointed out, even if they were, in fact, stockbrokers. Indeed, I was perfectly willing to stretch a point—anyone with a beard I intended to identify as Donald Barthelme, *The New Yorker* short-story writer.

"At Elaine's, the desirable places are what people in the know refer to as 'the line'—perhaps ten tables in a row. When we arrived, I took a quick glance at the line: The sudden fancy crossed my mind that Madame Tussaud herself had been working for a week to get it set up for ourselves and the Spinellis. At the first table, just by the front door, Kurt Vonnegut was sitting with his wife, the photographer Jill Krementz. With them was an older man who looked vaguely like the great novelist James T. Farrell. 'Kurt,' I said. I pushed Mr. Spinelli forward. 'Kurt, this is Jerry Spinelli, from Philadelphia. Jerry, Kurt Vonnegut.' I took a chance. 'Jerry, may I present James T. Farrell. This is Jerry Spinelli from Philly.'

"'Mr. Farrell' looked somewhat bewildered.

"I introduced Jill Krementz, and we moved on to the next table.

"Irwin Shaw was sitting there with Willie Morris, the former

EVERYONE COMES TO ELAINE'S

editor of *Harper's*, and the novelist Winston Groom. I introduced Spinelli to the table; there were pleasant nods and handshakes all around. At the next table, we paused to introduce ourselves to Gay Talese, who had just published *Thy Neighbor's Wife*, and A. E. Hotchner, the author of *Papa Hemingway*. 'Mr. Talese, Mr. Hotchner, may I present Jerry Spinelli, the writer from Philadelphia.' When he heard me introducing him as 'the writer from Philadelphia,' Mr. Spinelli beamed. We moved on to Bruce Jay Friedman, sitting with a large crowd. 'Bruce, Mr. Spinelli, the writer from Philadelphia.' Bruce rose and presented Mr. Spinelli to his friends.

"We were approaching—very slowly because of all the bowing and introductions—the most famous table at Elaine's . . . the one just beyond the side door that leads out to the kitchen and the Siberian reaches of the restaurant out back. Often the table is empty, with a plain white RESERVED sign on it; but when the sign is removed, the table is almost invariably occupied by Woody Allen and his entourage. It is an odd table to be the most desired. Not only is it immediately adjacent to the ebb and flow of Elaine's waiters as they rush back and forth from the kitchens but it is also just off the path of those forlorn people being herded into the back room—what is officially referred to as the Paul Desmond room, because the famous musician liked the quiet there. Not only that, but the Allen table is on the route to the restrooms; the traffic is considerable, the main reason being to table-hop en route to and from. Thus, the Woody Allen table, on the periphery of all this, is a place where one is jostled constantly, trays of osso buco sail alarmingly overhead like dirigibles, and when Allen is there, people stand in the doorway to the Desmond room and stare.

*A*t Elaine's, there is one famous house rule. At a place where table-hopping and squeezing in at a table to join even the vaguest of friends—'Mind if I join you?'—is very much de rigueur, it is *not* done at Woody Allen's table. Even on the way to the Gents, nothing more than a side glance at the brooding figure of Woody Allen, mournfully glancing down at his chicken francese, which I am told is his favorite dish, is permissible. To interrupt his meal by leaning over and calling out 'Hiya, Woody, how's it going?' would be unheard of.

"All of this was very much on my mind as our little band approached the Allen table, where the actor-writer was indeed in residence with a number of his friends. My first inclination was to stick to protocol and pass up his table to move on toward the far corner of the restaurant, where I spotted Peter Stone, Dan Jenkins, Herb Sargent, Michael Arlen, and others available for introductions.

"But I thought of Spinelli's four hundred and twenty-five dollars, and the long trip up on Amtrak, and the five dollars left in the savings account, and the half-finished manuscript in his typewriter-paper cardboard box.

"'Woody,' I said, 'forgive me. This is Jerry Spinelli, the writer from Philadelphia.'

"Woody looked up slowly. It was done very dramatically, as if he were looking up from under the brim of a large hat.

"'Yes,' he said evenly. 'I know.'

"We stood there transfixed. Allen gazed at us briefly, and then he returned to his contemplation of the chicken francese on his plate.

"We moved on to our table. As I recollect, we skipped Peter Stone, Michael Arlen, and the other luminaries in the corner. Jerry Spinelli wanted to talk. He was beside himself. His face shone. He

To interrupt his meal by leaning over and calling out "Hiya, Woody, how's it going?" would be unheard of.

was not quite sure what had happened. 'Did you hear *that*?' he asked. 'Jesus *Christ*!' He ordered a bottle of Soave wine. He brandished a fork and spoke about Kafka. He asked about agents. He told us a little about his novel, which was about the life of a young boy. He wanted to know if Harper and Row was a good house. In the midst of his euphoria, his wife, Eileen, turned to me. 'We've done a terrible thing,' she whispered to me. 'He's going to be unbearable. We've *spoiled* him!'

"Some months later, I received a letter from Jerry Spinelli. He was writing to tell me that his children's novel, *Space Station*, had been published by Little, Brown. It was a cheerful, chatty letter. Though he did not mention it, I knew he would want me to give his best regards to the gang up at Elaine's."

In the intervening years, George's protégé has written a slew of children's books with such titles as *Do the Funky Pickle, There's a Girl in My Hammerlock, Knots in My Yo-Yo String,* and *Maniac Magee,* which won the Newbery Medal.

A section of the wall at Elaine's

The first night I walked into Elaine's, I felt intimidated. This was 1980. I was a punk sportswriter for the *New York Post*, and there, on the wall, hung a slew of autographed book jackets culled from the pantheon of my youth: Gay Talese and Nick Pileggi, Norman Mailer and Peter Maas, Terry Southern and Irwin Shaw. Next to them, I saw frayed posters from *The Paris Review*, donated by George Plimpton, vying for space with original prints and photographs from the owner's pet artists: Warhol and Jamie Wyeth, Harry Benson, Neil Leifer. On a shelf in the front room, a facsimile of an Oscar statuette stood amid photos of Elaine Kaufman with assorted Hollywood mandarins. I'd slaked many a thirst in newspaper saloons like Costello's, the White Horse Tavern, and, of course, the Lion's Head on Christopher Street, where Jessica Lange used to sling fried calamari as the Clancy Brothers jigged in the back room for Pete Hamill, the boxing scribe Mike "Wolfman" Katz, and the actor Ed

Harris, stopping by on his way home from the Circle Rep. But Elaine's? David Halberstam's ultimate writers club? Jeez, this joint was forbidding. Cliquish. Uptown. But not uptown enough to make make me pass on thirteen thousand dollars—the amount my agent was holding for me. He was throwing a book party and said come and get it.

I walked through the door, grabbed the check, counted the zeros, found a dark corner and started inhaling Budweisers and the scene. I spoke to no one until a stocky woman in a floral-print dress plunked down next to me. I'd caught her eyeing me earlier, so I stuck out my hand and said, "Hi, I'm one of Jay Kanter's clients—" She cut me off. "I know who you are." She had a raspy voice and what Willie Morris, who devoted an entire chapter of his autobiography to the restaurant, described as a "curly smile." She said, "I saw you pick up thirteen grand when you walked in here, which means you're working. I've watched you tip my bartender two bucks on every drink. My name's Elaine, and you're welcome in my place anytime." Talk about an icebreaker.

Despite the wee hour, there was a raucous rhythm to the crowd swaying two-deep at the bar—a bar, I must add, serving grown-up cocktails. Elaine's adheres to Twain's dictum that whiskey is for drinking and water is for fighting over, and any visitor ordering Evian or white wine spritzers or, Lord forbid, one of those fruity cosmopolitans had best be prepared to go thirsty or, in extremis, be shown the door. From the stereo speakers above the crashing bodies, Junior Walker laced a saxophone riff sharp enough to cut falling silk. Then came Piaf. And though it was midweek, each time a shadow crossed the vestibule, heads surreptitiously swiveled, eager to catch whatever big shot might be bouncing in next.

—BOB DRURY, *journalist*

" Jackie Gleason came in one night, this is a short time before he died, and he went behind the bar and did a hilarious turn as Joe the Bartender. It was an incredible performance that had all of us rolling off our chairs. But when he went home, everyone sat around and cried. "

—ELAINE

Everyone Comes to Elaine's

11

Jackie Gleason on the night
he was "Joe the Bartender"

*I was so afraid
I wouldn't
wake up in time
to let the crew
in that I slept in
the window of
the restaurant.*

As celebrities from all over were gravitating
to the unpretentious place on Second Avenue, the
movies took notice and over the years Elaine and her
establishment have appeared in more than a dozen
films. Woody Allen's film *Manhattan* opens with a full-screen shot
of the restaurant's front window. "When Woody shot the scene,"
Elaine says, "I was so afraid I wouldn't wake up in time to let the
crew in that I slept in the window of the restaurant."

In the movie *Network*, directed by Sidney Lumet, who is one of
Elaine's regulars, William Holden and Faye Dunaway have dinner
in Elaine's. There is also a scene in *Diary of a Mad Housewife* that
was shot in Elaine's, as well as scenes in *Author! Author!* and *The
Odd Couple*, among others.

Elaine herself has also appeared in a few of the films.

"Back in 1969, when I was still in the movie business," the
writer Dominick Dunne says, "I cast Elaine for a bit part in the
movie version of Mart Crowley's famous play *The Boys in the Band*.
She was hilarious. She completely stole the scene. She got the
movie off to a rollicking good start."

"I was Al Pacino's personal manager," the producer Marty
Bregman says, "at the time *The Godfather* was such a thunderous
blockbuster. Overnight, Pacino had become a superstar and, being
who he is, he was very nervous and rather frightened about his el-
evated celebrity status. I was going to dinner with Al and Diane
Keaton, who was already a big name, and Al wanted to be sure that
we went somewhere where he would not be bothered. His life had
already become celebrity hell.

"I said, 'I know just the place, I've been going there for years
and celebrities are never hassled. Nobody will bother you, trust

me.' So we settle in at a table at Elaine's and we are listening to the waiter's recitation of the specials when I notice, at a table two down from us, a trio of ladies who are intently looking our way. And gesturing in our direction. I look around for Elaine for protection, but she is nowhere to be seen. Meanwhile, I can hear one of the ladies, plump and eager, saying, 'That's him! Oh, I'm sure that's him!' I don't know what to do. Should I perform a preemptive strike by anticipating their advance to our table and intercept them? Should I make an emergency tour of the restaurant to find Elaine? Should I ignore them and hope for the best?

"The plump woman has already unraveled herself from her chair and is on her way over to our table, a look on her face that can only mean trouble for Marty Bregman who has obviously led his star client into a celebrity trap. Trust me, hah! The woman is at our table, leaning in on us, with a look on her face like she's just found treasure on the Second Avenue sidewalk.

"'Marty! Marty!' she exclaims. 'You are Marty Bregman, aren't you? Remember me? Evander Childs High School? You directed us in the senior class play. I was Blanche, remember?' I stood up. She gave me a rib-cracking bear hug accompanied by high-decibel giggles. Whereupon she returned to her table, totally ignoring Al and Diane."

There *was another* Godfather *incident at Elaine's.* Frank Sinatra, and the author of *The Godfather*, Mario Puzo, were both there one night, at separate tables. They had never met, but in the book the singer named Johnny Fontane had been assumed by many people to be based on Sinatra. "Before the book came out," Puzo wrote at the time, "my publisher

Frank Sinatra enjoyed Elaine's but not when Mario Puzo was there

got a letter from Sinatra's lawyers demanding to see the manuscript. In polite language we refused. However, the movie was another story. In the initial conferences with Paramount's legal staff they showed concern about this until I reassured them the part was very minor in the film.

"Now the thing was, in my book, I had written the Fontane character with complete sympathy for the man and his lifestyle and his hang-ups. I thought I had caught the innocence of great showbiz people, their despair at the corruption their kind of life forces on them and the people around them. I thought I had caught the inner innocence of the character. But I could also see that if Sinatra thought the character was himself, he might not like it—the book—or me.

"But of course some people wanted to bring us together. So that night we were both at Elaine's, and Elaine asked if I would object to meeting Sinatra. I said it was okay with me if it was okay with him. It was not okay with Sinatra. 'Keep him away from me,' he said. And that was perfectly okay with me. I didn't give it another thought.

A year later I was working on the movie script in Hollywood. I rarely went out in the evening but this particular night I was invited to my producer's friend's birthday party at Chasen's. A party for twelve given by a famous millionaire. As we were having a drink at the bar, he said Sinatra was having dinner at another table and would I like to meet him. I said no, but the millionaire took me by the hand and started leading me toward a table. 'You gotta meet Frank,' the millionaire said. 'He's a good friend of mine.'

"'I'd like you to meet my good friend Mario Puzo,' said the millionaire.

"'I don't think so,' Sinatra said.

"Which sent me on my way. But the poor millionaire didn't get the message. He started over again.

"'I don't want to meet him,' Sinatra said.

"Meanwhile, I was trying to get the hell out of there, but I heard the millionaire stuttering his apologies, not to me, but to

Elaine asked if I would object to meeting Sinatra. I said it was okay with me if it was okay with him. It was not okay with Sinatra.

Sinatra. The millionaire was actually in tears. 'Frank, I'm sorry. God, Frank, I didn't know, Frank, I'm sorry . . . '

"'It's not your fault,' Sinatra said.

"I always run away from an argument and I have rarely in my life been disgusted by anything human beings do, but after that I said to Sinatra, 'Listen, it wasn't my idea.'

This was roughly equivalent to Einstein pulling a knife on Al Capone. It just wasn't done.

"And then the most astounding thing happened. He completely misunderstood. He thought I was apologizing for the character of Johnny Fontane in my book.

"He said, and his voice was almost kind, 'Who told you to put that in the book, your publisher?'

"I was completely dumbfounded. I don't let publishers put commas in my books. That's the only thing I have character about. Finally I said, 'I mean about being introduced to you.'

"Sinatra started to shout abuse. Contrary to his reputation, he did not use foul language. The worst thing he called me was a pimp, which rather flattered me since I've never been able to get girl-friends to squeeze blackheads out of my back much less hustle for me. I do remember his saying that if I hadn't been so much older than he was, he would have beat the hell out of me. I was a kid when he was singing at the Paramount, but okay, he looked twenty years younger. But what hurt was that here he was, a northern Italian, threatening me, a southern Italian, with physical violence. This was roughly equivalent to Einstein pulling a knife on Al Capone. It just wasn't done. Northern Italians never mess with southern Italians, except to get them put in jail or deported to some desert island.

"Sinatra kept up his abuse and I kept staring at him. He kept staring down at his plate. Yelling. He never looked up. Finally I walked away and out of the restaurant. My humiliation must have showed on my face because he yelled at me, 'Choke. Go ahead and choke.' The voice frenzied, high-pitched.

"So he leveled me twice—once at Elaine's and again at Chasen's."

The first time Sylvester Stallone came in," the bartender Tommy Carney says, "was the *Rocky* days, and he had his body-guards with him—he always had bodyguards. We'd have presidents and heads of state in here, and he'd be the only one with bodyguards. So this first time he came in, he was wearing a long leather trench coat. Elaine walked up to him and said, 'It's very nice to meet you. Welcome to the restaurant.' He took his coat off and was looking all around and Elaine said, 'What's the problem?' and he said, 'Where do I put my coat?' and Elaine pointed to the hooks on the wall and said, "You hang your coat up right there.' He waits, 'But this is a very good coat, I can't hang my coat up there.' At that point Elaine lost a little patience and said, 'Why, is it the only coat you have?'"

Another bartender, Brian MacDonald, recalls "the humid night Bill Clinton was nominated as the party's candidate. The city had decided to repave Second Avenue, and even though limousines and taxis had to drop the patrons off blocks away, the joint was completely packed. At one point I looked out the window as a large yellow machine with flashing lights crawled past, spreading new tar on the road. Steam rose from the street and men in yellow vulcanized suits with hoods and goggles walked alongside the hulking mass in a scene straight out of *The Terminator*. As I watched, a large, muscular man emerged from the vapors and approached the door. Sure enough, it was Arnold Schwarzenegger himself, coming to join the revelers. I remember thinking then that the Terminator and Elaine—who was sitting at table four, surrounded by power brokers and the press—have at least one thing in common: They are terrific survivors."

I *seat Hollywood people carefully," Elaine says, "ever* since I put a couple of macho producers at adjoining tables and they wound up slinging calamari at each other. There was also the time the Hollywood producer Bob Evans and his current wife had booked a table on the same night as two of his ex-wives, Ali Mac-Graw and Phyllis George, who was there with her husband, John Brown, the governor of Kentucky. I didn't know what to do, how it would all go down. I put them at three different places in the restaurant, hoping they wouldn't see one another, but Ali came with her seven-year-old son—Evans was his father—who went around the restaurant kissing his step-mommies. It turned out just fine. After the kid broke the ice, they all got together and had a fine time."

I put a couple of macho producers at adjoining tables and they wound up slinging calamari at each other.

When an aging movie starlet ordered a salad and a glass of water for dinner one night, explaining that she had to keep an eye on her figure, Elaine, who frowns upon such niggling dinner fare, said, "You're the only one who does."

"The Hollywood people are cute, sometimes funny, and what the hell, they pay the rent," Elaine says, "but I don't have time for that silliness. The Hollywood part of it is the same wherever they go. It doesn't make any difference where you put somebody from Hollywood. I mean, you let him come in because he's funny. He's an entity unto himself. He's the epitome of mediocrity, the Hollywood bird. I guarantee you they're going to be funny. It's the funniest end of the money business. It's unreal. I mean, I feel kind of sorry for them. They live in those California houses and they act like they're suburbia, and they're cuckoo. I mean, they're part of a corporate master plan and they don't admit to it, and they have to go home early because otherwise somebody will think they're unemployed. So they keep coming and saying, 'You should really open up a place out there.' I say, 'But everybody goes home early in Los Angeles, and what are we going to do when they go home? You can't even get a taxi out there.' And they're all worried that they don't get invited to the parties—they're sort of lying to each other all the time.

"In contrast to Hollywood, if you live in New York, it's a twenty-four-hour world, and the city adjusts to the way you are and you find your roots here for what you need, for what you have to give, and what you want to take. Very rarely can you find such an existence. I mean, if you find that it's better for you to wake up at four in the morning, you can find an existence that way, and a whole society working, and it would make you no less a person of

I *love it when she sits at my table* when I'm in the restaurant. She likes to laugh, and she likes to dish, and I'm a willing partner in both categories. This lady is a New York presence of very high wattage. She is part of the lore of the city. She is a player in its social history, with landmark status, like Mrs. Astor. Way down the road, when her time comes, I'll bet money she makes the front page of the *New York Times*.

—DOMINICK DUNNE, author

character to prefer to live like that. And it's just as well to go to sleep at four as it is to get up at four. The city is like clay, it molds to you. That's what's nice about it. It's the greatest incentive city. I mean, it's very hard to stay still in New York. You have to move."

Harvey Weinstein's Miramax *is one of the few film* companies headquartered in New York. "I have been stopping by and enjoying myself at Elaine's for over thirty years," he says. "My dad, Max, once joined my brother Bob and me there—he considered it a big night out. Sentimentally, we will always be attached to this wonderful bistro. Elaine's is New York at its most unique and at its best. If Damon Runyon were alive he'd have a corner table. When the stars of our films come in from the Coast, Elaine's is where they want us to take them."

"The thing about Elaine's," says *Harper's* editor, Lewis Lapham, "is that nobody will allow himself to be impressed by anybody. You could say I just sold seventeen thousand copies of my book today and someone would ask what you did yesterday."

"No matter what you've done," Joan Rivers says, "or where you've been or who you're with, you come into Elaine's and nobody turns to stare. I've gone in there after a costume party when I've been wearing a Minnie Mouse dress and Minnie Mouse ears. I've gone there after the most formal, stuffy charity dinner parties. I've also gone there on a Memorial Day weekend Sunday night, when I just had two flat tires on my way in from Connecticut and I'm a bloody mess in jeans and no makeup and oil-stained shirt. Nobody gives you a second look.

"When a friend of mine, Hester Mundez, who's a writer with a great sense of humor, got engaged, she wanted me to meet her fiancé, Ron, who, she said, was nineteen years her junior and a bit of an eccentric. She asked, Where do you want to go to dinner to meet him? And I said, Elaine's. So I was waiting for them at Elaine's when in walked nineteen-year-old Ron with his thirty-eight-year-old fiancée, he in a full Dracula cape lined in red and a beanie hat with a propeller on it. Nobody but nobody in Elaine's blinked or turned around. That's Elaine's for you."

"One night at Elaine's," says Morgan Entrekin, "my high school friend Johnny Bransford and I got into an argument over who could run faster. After going back and forth for a while, I said, Why don't we just go settle it now. We made a wager; by this time others had heard so people placed bets on one or the other of us. At midnight, we left Elaine's with a crowd, went to the Central Park reservoir, paced off a hundred yards, took off our shoes, and raced. It was January, about ten degrees outside. Johnny was fast, but I was faster. I returned to Elaine's to a triumphant welcome. A spontaneous celebration."

We left Elaine's with a crowd, went to the Central Park reservoir, paced off a hundred yards, took off our shoes, and raced.

*T*ony Bennett, who paints almost as well as he sings, says, "I live in a world of musicians and songwriters and show business people, which is okay as far as it goes, but I relish going to Elaine's because I get to visit with intellectual people, especially the writers, and Elaine herself is a refreshing change from the people in my everyday life. Last time I was in the place, while she was visiting at my table, I sketched a little pencil portrait of her. She was delighted with it, framed it, and hung it over the bar. That's like getting a curtain call."

The artist Jamie Wyeth has also had his portrait of Elaine

Tony Bennett drawing

framed and hung on the wall. "I have been a habitué of Elaine's for many years," he confesses, "and, quite simply, I am in love with Elaine. Her wise counsel, her no-bullshit opinions of people and events I value a lot. Through the years I have lived for periods in New York, mostly to paint portraits; many of these portraits had their genesis at Elaine's. My two years of intense study and painting of Rudolf Nureyev was triggered by having dined with him at Elaine's. While sharing a studio with Andy Warhol we often ended our evenings at Elaine's. Over those years I harbored a secret desire to paint Elaine. I wanted to make a record, in paint, of this colossus

Jamie Wyeth painting

of New York life. The opportunity finally arose when Elaine mentioned her saloon's thirtieth anniversary. Would I do a sketch of her? she asked. I leaped at the chance, immediately setting up my studio in her off room—the saloon's Siberia. With that done, I soon entered a rarely seen, never explored world—Elaine in daylight. That world usually began at eleven A.M. Having shuttered her bar at three or four in the morning, she would return midday to count the previous night's receipts, balance the books, order food, restock spirits, and sample new entrées. She would remain at this for two to three hours, during which time I feverishly painted. Between table checks, wine orders, and phone calls she would pose for me. The resulting painting portrays Elaine seated at one of her starched white-tablecloth round tables, staring directly at the viewer, a book in one hand and a fork in the other. This was my attempt at an official portrait of the doyenne of New York literary hangouts. When I last visited Elaine's, the completed portrait hung on the wall, and it had become the menu cover."

A

fter midnight one sultry summer evening in 1981," says the artist LeRoy Neiman, "Lee Majors and I, following our duties as judges of the Miss New York State Beauty Pageant, were out on the town. As tradition has it, a stop at Elaine's was in order.

"Seated at the table next to ours was a striking figure wearing a Russian cap. As I frequently do in public situations, once a compelling figure or something extraordinary comes into my direct line of vision, I pulled out a pen, and, while Lee and I chatted, rapidly sketched the subject, a highly recognizable Rudolf Nureyev. While

I was sketching, he was complaining that he was chilled by the air conditioning. Then, taking matters into his own hands, he pulled one of Elaine's checkered tablecloths off a table and wrapped it around his shoulders with a flourish.

"It soon became evident to him that he was the focus of my work and a conversation ensued. When the sketch was finished,

LeRoy Neiman's sketch of Nureyev

Lee was keen for a copy, and my subject responded to it with great enthusiasm as well, remarking that I'd caught the Tartar in him. I asked him if he'd sign the drawing, and he graciously complied, requesting that a copy be sent to his New York address at the Dakota.

"That same evening, after Nureyev departed, I did a sketch of Elaine."

Neiman's sketch of Elaine

An Ode to Elaine's, Circa 1980

I met Eubie Blake in Elaine's once,
And Eubie Blake met me.
All kinds of entertainments
In there for free.

Yes, the check is expensive,
But the owner has noticed your piece
On the art of Señor Wences,
Who is having the veal with Ed Meese.

How many restaurateurs see
Bylines? And how many joints
Feature Prince Sihanouk, Galli-Curci,
And Pelé discussing gross points?

Or Margaret Mead, Irving "Swifty" Lazar,
And several girls in grass skirts
Conferring in some kind of foreign
Tongue with Herblock and Vic Wertz?

Where else but Elaine's do they welcome
Writers, again and again?
Remember the night that Malcolm
X and Solzhenitsyn came in?

Abbie Hoffman and Yuri Andropov,
When they were underground,
Stopped by in the hope of
Finding someone around.

They sat down with Mantle and Maris
And me. It was three A.M.
Yuri told some hellacious stories.
I think it was him.

Myself, the Who, Jerry Wexler, and Ethel
Waters or Rosenberg, one,
Said, "Let's do a network special!"
One night, but it never got done.

Was it Vine Deloria Jr.
Or some multimedia cop
Who ordered the pasta with tuna
And undid Diana Dors' top?

And was it Felix Rohatyn
With Alain Robbe-Grillet?
I do know that Ed Bulwer-Lytton
And I were three tables away.

Then once I had fried calamari
With the board of PEN,
A midget from E.T. who was very
Drunk, and the Hollywood Ten.

Why go where the waiters don't know you?
The late scrambled eggs are just right.
Cher. Cuomo. Alfonso Bedoya.
And so on into the night.

—Roy Blount Jr.

" As for our menu, food can have some very high points and some very low points at different times. The difficult thing is getting consistency. My chef is incredible, but on a day he doesn't feel so hot, you could kill yourself. So I try to keep the food simple and try to keep to a pure form. I serve Italian rather than French because, although personally I like French food, I think a true French kitchen in America is impossible. **"**

—ELAINE

Everyone Comes to Elaine's

12

Actor Peter Boyle

PHOTOGRAPH BY JONATHAN BECKER

M any of Elaine's now accomplished authors fondly recall their initiation into Elaine's privileged membership. Stuart Woods is a prolific bestselling author who has featured Elaine as a character in a number of his mystery novels. "He gets my sound better than anyone else," Elaine says.

"In the late eighties I wrote a novel called *New York Dead*," Woods says, "featuring a protagonist named Stone Barrington. The first paragraph read, 'Elaine's, late.' To my surprise, it became the first of a series, which now numbers ten, one third of my oeuvre, and Elaine has now become one of my richer fictional characters. She likes this, and I get good tables. Also, a poster of one of my book jackets occupies a place of honor, I am reliably informed, in the number one stall of the ladies' room.

"No dialogue I could invent for her, though, comes up to the standard of the original, which is minimalist and to the point:

"Waiter: 'Elaine would like to buy you an after-dinner drink.'

"Me: 'A double Bailey's, please.'

"Elaine: 'Single!'

"Elaine is renowned for her largesse with struggling writers and her attention to detail with the spending habits of those she deems to have made it. One night, another old customer of Elaine's and I had been to a black-tie dinner earlier, and we stopped by for a drink, taking a table in the back. Elaine came over. 'You fuckin' rich guys,' she said pleasantly, 'are always having dinner somewhere else, then comin' in here and takin' up a table!' Such is the warmth of her greeting.

"My readers are always writing to me to ask how they can get a good table at Elaine's. Elaine's reply to this question is, 'I take

A scholarly-looking girl with a short skirt and incredibly beautiful legs danced atop a jukebox adjacent to the front door.

reservations.' My advice is, go three times a week for two years, and you're in. She likes regulars.

"All you really need to know is, Elaine's is not so much a restaurant as a club, where the public is allowed to pay to watch the members eat, and the members like that."

My first visit to Elaine's could have served as the pencil sketch for a fully realized portrait of the nights to come," Bruce Jay Friedman says. "A scholarly-looking girl with a short skirt and incredibly beautiful legs danced atop a jukebox adjacent to the front door. Off in another world, a novelist at the back end of the restaurant played jazz chords on a piano, making tortured faces as if the music was being wrenched out of his soul, which it may or may not have been. The lighting was safe and comforting. It had always been one of the restaurant's secrets. Alongside a bank of phones, a crap game was discreetly under way, presided over by a man named Mosely, whose specialization was to make loans to writers who were short of funds, which they generally were. He was in no rush to be repaid.

"'I never worry,' he would say, 'so long as they don't avoit my eyes.'

"When a writer's credit was no longer good with Mosely, there was always Elaine, who kept a substantial amount of cash tucked away in her décolletage and was quick to reach into it when a writer needed financial support. No repayments were required. She had always had a congenital crush on writers as a group. Among her House Rules: Never borrow money from a novelist.

"That first night at Elaine's, I ordered a dish that was highly satisfying and that I was to enjoy many times—though it eventually led to an annual query from my accountant: 'I don't understand this eighteen-thousand-dollar item for veal piccata.' Over the many years, I've had only a single bumpy experience with the food. One night, I noticed that kidneys, a favorite of mine, were listed on the menu. I'd always had them breaded. These were on the rare side and prepared in a style that was unusual for me. I had trouble getting past the first bite and thought I would discreetly deposit it in my napkin. Elaine, who had been watching, said, 'A Frenchman could've kept 'em down.'

She had always had a congenital crush on writers as a group. Among her House Rules: Never borrow money from a novelist.

"Arthur Kopit, who wrote *Nine*, came by with the hopelessly beautiful artist Priscilla Bowden. As a couple, they were unbearably attractive. To compound the felony, Barbara Harris, another heartbreaker, was starring in Kopit's hit play *Oh Dad, Poor Dad . . .* I found all of this perfection inexcusable. For solace, I went plunging into a blackjack game with a young investment banker from Southampton. Within a short period of time, I had won several thousand dollars, which normally would have been cause for celebration. But I did not know if gambling debts, cavalierly incurred at Elaine's, were honored—some were, some weren't—and could not see myself sending 'representatives' to break my new friend's legs. As a result, I could not relax until I had lost it all back.

"The combination of wine, women, gambling, and Mediterranean waiters who outdid the writers in sensitivity was combustible. To drain off energy that had not gone into the day's—or month's—output of prose and poetry, there was arm wrestling and midnight competitive sprints down Second Avenue. When the director James Toback began to lag behind in a push-up contest, Elaine said, 'Put a broad under him.'

"Late that first night, as if by heavenly intervention, I found myself taking home the girl who had danced so invitingly atop the jukebox. Though she was never to repeat the performance, I no longer doubted that I had found the ultimate hangout.

"The nights all seemed glittering and carefree. There wasn't much literary content to them. Presumably, some writing transpired during the daylight hours. But how remarkable that such a safe haven existed. To know that there *was* such a place. That there would always be a party, one to which there was a permanent invitation. Where there was no need to slink around nibbling at hors d'oeuvres, and wondering snobbishly if anyone spoke the same language. Was there a downside to all of this, an *Anna Karenina* that

Writer Bruce Jay Friedman

PHOTOGRAPH BY JESSICA BURSTEIN

159

went unwritten because of those dissolute midnight hours? Those who saw such a danger went off to teach writing workshops in the Midwest. Others stayed behind, stole some bleary-eyed pleasure after a good day's work—or as often a bad day's work. Many published. Few perished. The output from the virtuous hinterlands was less than torrential.

"Everyone seemed young and either strong or formidably dissipated. The cast slowly began to change. Or did this happen overnight? William Styron gave way to George Steinbrenner, Irwin Shaw to Harvey Weinstein. There was less of Mailer, more of Miramax. A wave of film people appeared, most of them named Marty. Being in what they thought was a literary atmosphere made them feel literary and spared them the trouble of actually reading literature. Or perhaps they solved the mystery of how writers got by with so little. And devised plans to pay them even less. Models and actors followed in their wake. Al Pacino, thinking I'd be flattered, stopped and said he'd read the 'coverage' of my new novel. I promised to review the 'coverage' of his next performance. The restaurant caught fire with law enforcers. It raised a question. Was it preferable to spend an evening with a poet or a homicide detective? A second room had to be added, and there was some grumbling about the change in the very character of the restaurant. Had the faith been broken? Why couldn't Elaine's have remained a secret hideaway for sensitive and for the most part impoverished fiction writers.

"There was always the fascination of the front door. Who would be the next to slip through. Even the most jaded contributor to *Lingua Franca* snapped to weary attention when Frank Sinatra came barreling in, with Truffaut slipping quietly in behind him.

Elaine herself, who had entertained royalty, came girlishly apart when Marlon Brando appeared—or materialized—before her.

"It was the sports stars that threw me off stride. 'Would you mind if Dominguin joined you? Can you make a little room for Jim Brown? Hi, I'm Derek Jeter.'

"There was a moment that seems out of time when I walked the Midtown streets at night and stopped to look in, or actually peer in, the great windows of several gentlemen's clubs, the chandeliered ceilings, the wood-paneled rooms, the affluent-looking pipe-smoking men in overstuffed chairs, sipping brandy, appearing to read Thackeray, or, more likely, the *Financial Times*. I wondered why I had no such club of my own. And then I realized that I was on my way to Elaine's, and that I had an unofficial membership in the most unique and convivial club the city has ever known."

It was the sports stars that threw me off stride. "Would you mind if Dominguin joined you? Can you make a little room for Jim Brown? Hi, I'm Derek Jeter."

The writer Terry Southern, in his own inimitable way, remembered his baptism at Elaine's: "My first visit to the Great El's must have been with 'Gamblin' Jack' Richardson, since, if memory serves, he was the first person allowed to run a tab there. Soon everybody was running one. El had about twelve customers her opening year, and I don't know how she made ends meet. Some say a handsome Latino lover was bankrolling the El. Anyway, everyone would argue over the check.

"'I'll get it!' Jack would declare, adding in his grandest manner, 'More wine for my friends!'

"'No, no,' the editor Coco Brown—another big spender—would insist. 'I'll get it! Drinks all around!'

"But nobody was getting anything, because everyone was running a tab. I once nursed a tab along seven years. I still have the bill, in the form of an ordinary dinner check, although the total had been incurred in a single evening: Feb. 10, 1972. $278.65, and then, scrawled boldly beneath it, *Nada* on this tab since 1965! What're you, some kind of wiseacre?!?! El. A paltry sum, to be sure, compared with those of others one might name—Peter Beard, *par exemple.* He strung on out for five thou. We're talking five *big ones*, mister! He was just back from the Kenya bush and was keen to square himself at El's.

"'The last personal check I gave her,' he said with a chuckle, 'proved to be of a highly *resilient* nature—I think I better take cash.' So we stopped at a bank.

"'Get it in twenties,' I suggested, 'and we may see some action flashing the roll.'

"In the cab heading uptown, Pete tossed the wad about with great glee. Strictly a C-note man himself, he was doubtless amused to see so many small bills together at one time.

"We got there before El arrived, so we didn't have to relinquish the big roll quite yet.

"'Let me carry the roll for a while,' I suggested. 'Maybe I can score celeb or teeny poon with it.'

"Pete agreed, but before we could settle down, who should appear at the front but Coco Brown with an ultra-fab on each arm. I asked Peter to low-profile it while I invited Coco—whose plans were always fairly flexible—to join me, and then for Pete to come to the table and ask to borrow a thou. So as soon as Coco and the nifties were seated, he did.

"'Gosh, Pete,' I complained, 'you haven't paid back the thou I gave you this morning,' but I dutifully peeled off—yet another!—

thou for him. Coco's astonishment was absolute, and it was twofold: one, that a certain yours truly could so casually lay out two big ones in a single day, and two, that 'Bush Boss' Beard hadn't hit up Capote, Cavett, or one of the Kennedy swells he hung with instead of a chronic ne'er-do-well. In any case, the nifties were duly impressed, and when El arrived, they obliquely sounded her out as to my overall 'Mister Right' qualifications.

"'You're barking up the wrong eucalyptus, sister,' quipped El as she counted the twenties and stashed them in the wondrous depths of her décolletage. 'The guy's a deadbeat, a loner, a one-nighter, and he's strictly out for poon . . . and so's his sidekick.'

Producer Dick Wolf and writer Joseph Heller

PHOTOGRAPH BY JESSICA BURSTEIN

"And as the girls demurely withdrew from the table, she gave them one of her internationally famous 'Great El Zingers': 'And that goes double for the other stiff you're sitting with.'

"It was all in jest, of course, but how were the ultra-fabs to know—percipience in these matters hardly being their long suit?

"Some years later, I asked El if she remembered the incident, hoping guilt might cause her to spring for a couple of rounds. But she wasn't too visibly moved.

"'Sure, I remember,' she said with a guffaw. 'It knocked you three jokers *right out of the box*,' adding with her boss-charm smile and twinkle of mischief, 'if you'll pardon my *français*.'"

Roy Blount Jr., one of this country's great humorists: "I fondly remember nights at Elaine's, in the seventies, with Dan Jenkins, Bud Shrake, Bruce Friedman, and various others, that went on until daylight sometimes. The best scrambled eggs I ever had was one night at Elaine's in the wee hours, when Elaine scrambled them herself. People may complain all they wish about Elaine's cuisine, but every time I scramble eggs, I remember those eggs. I've never been able to get them that fluffy yet substantial.

"One night Elaine seated me with a party including Peter Boyle, who had just done 'Dueling Brandos' with John Belushi—trading bits of 'I coulda been a contender' and all that, back and forth, to the tune of 'Dueling Banjos'—on *Saturday Night Live*. Boyle kept trying to compliment me on something in *Esquire* that had in fact been written by Taylor Branch, and I kept trying to assure him that his part in 'Dueling Brandos' would guarantee him immortality if he never did anything else the rest of his life, which didn't gratify him much. Still, I enjoyed the conversation. For some reason I had driven to Elaine's that night. When, on my way home at four A.M. or so, I was stopped by the police somewhere deep in Harlem—I had made a wrong turn, kept wondering where Central Park had gone to—I was in no condition to be operating a motor vehicle, I'm afraid, but was still in such a convivial mood that I started telling the cop about my chat with Boyle. The cop responded by doing *his* Brando, which wasn't half bad. As good as Boyle's, I told the cop. If he never did anything else in life . . . He pointed me west and let me go.

"Another night I was trading experiences with a very funny guy whose name I hadn't caught, when it suddenly hit me who he was—an icon of the sixties, on the lam at the time. 'You're Abbie Hoffman!' I exclaimed, probably even more loudly than I realized, and I still remember the happily delinquent, quintessentially American grin on his surgically altered face.

*T*he Italian matinee idol, Vittorio Gassman, came in for dinner one night and at his invitation I sat down to join him. He had veal and pasta, espresso, and then wanted to know if we had flan, which was a favorite of his. Indeed we did, because it is also a favorite of mine. The flan was brought to the table, and then rising so all could see, he raised the plate and in one gesture sucked up the whole thing. Got a great round of applause.

—ELAINE

"Nora Ephron and I spent a good deal of time trying to adapt Ron Rosenbaum's novel *Murder at Elaine's* into a musical. The novel, which ran serially in *High Times*, had been inspired by the coup that took *New York* magazine away from its editor, Clay Felker. There would have been some great numbers. A character based loosely on Felker—we had in mind Charles Durning—was to sing 'When I'm Good and Dead,' about how all the people who deplored him in life would remember him fondly in memoriam. A crazy old right-wing rich guy, the father of the male lead, was going to sing 'The Big Nuts Rise to the Top,' the *Times*'s science section having recently reported that in a can of mixed nuts the largest ones actually do make their way to the surface, for scientific reasons. There was going to be a dog character singing 'It's Hard to Be an Urban Dog.' And an Italian waiter's song: the specials, in *recitatif*, to media-gossip accompaniment. For various reasons, including the death of Howard Ashman, who was going to direct, it never came off. I don't know who could have carried off the part of Elaine herself."

T*hirty years ago," Michael Caine says, "I came to* America for the first time to do publicity for *Alfie*. I knew virtually no one but I met Bobby Zarem, the publicist, who took me to Elaine's and I immediately knew I had found a second home. No matter that I am miles older than she is, Elaine is mother. She is a mine of information—the first night I arrive in New York I go to Elaine's to see her and to find out where everybody is and to let everyone know I'm in the city. Elaine and I have a special relationship. On Saturdays she takes me to lunch for caviar at Petrossian's. I don't know why she decided on caviar lunches, but it certainly is a lovely way to spend a Saturday lunch. I have had her to my place in England, which indicates my family feeling for her because by nature I am not a convivial host.

"When I am in her restaurant, Elaine, knowing that I like the company of writers, has introduced me to Mailer and Woody and Tom Wolfe and Joseph Heller, the late great author of *Catch 22*, and Kurt Vonnegut, among many others, which has been wonderful for me. Half the people I know in New York I met at Elaine's.

"She always sits at my table but we never talk about film, rather about books and art and such, just as when she sits with writers she does not talk about books but about film and other things. She is wise, she is well versed, and she knows who is who and what is what and where all the bodies are buried."

Superstars of the ballet world come as regularly to Elaine's as the stars of Broadway and films. "Nureyev was one of my staunchest and most entertaining regulars," Elaine says. "Not only here, but there was a night in the late sixties when I was in London for a short vacation, and Rudy and I danced the night away at Anabelle's. I was not so heavy then and Rudy loved to dance rock and roll stuff. It was not his high point, however, being another kind of music and not his kind of dancing, but he was very enthusiastic and funny on the dance floor—swirled me around and wanted to do lifts but had to sort of fake it in view of my unballerinalike *avoir du pois*. It was a great London crowd— a couple of the Stones and Beatles were there—there was a disco up on top of the penthouse and we all went up there to hang out.

"Segue to my joint, it's a Sunday night and Rudy has come right from the airport with his suitcase to meet up with some friends of his. Rudy always checked in on his first night in New York. On this particular Sunday it happened that Misha Baryshnikov was also in the place, along with the choreographer-dancer Peter Martins, and other ballet people. They are at a table adjoining Rudy's.

"Champagne and vodka were flowing and Misha, feeling festive, picks up his chair and begins to dance with it as his partner, a fantastic dance, spins and lifts and God knows what. Peter gets up and starts doing counterbalance with him. Suddenly, not to be outdone, Rudy grabs his chair and dances a pas de deux. It was some wonderful scene, the greatest dancers in the world, whirling and twirling with their four-legged partners here at the bar, accompanied by Frank Sinatra singing 'Fly Me to the Moon.'"

In 1995, Gael Greene updated Elaine's for her readers:

DOES THE COSMIC ANGST OF THIS SALOON ado escape you? If your adrenaline is unmoved by minor masochism, if you're not susceptible to narcissistic mortification, if you have never quite understood hanging out, the literary locker room, the need to escape from your wife, the seven drinks before stuportime, the fear of closing your eyes, the terror of intimacy, the horror of being alone, then it is difficult to explain the spiritual imperative of a refuge like Elaine's. But twenty years from now, writer Michael Monney muses, "Some earnest Ph.D. candidate will do a literary history, digging through unpaid bar bills and old menus, to be published by

PHOTOGRAPH BY JESSICA BURSTEIN

Clint Eastwood on one of his regular visits

Viking Pompous Editions. How amusing. That Elaine Kaufman should be the Madame de Maintenon of the age."

The Beautiful People clotted there, light bouncing off perfect capped smiles, making midnight Second Avenue bright as noon. Limos double-parked in the grimy no-man's-land of way-uptown, vomiting stars, superstars—Mastroianni, Clint Eastwood, John Lennon, Lynda Bird with George Hamilton and her Secret Service shadow (they wanted a prime table—Elaine stood them at the jukebox), and the ultimate wow of the sixties, Jackie. Inevitably, in their wake, came the third-string royalty and the second-string rich, the politicians and flacks, the sycophants, the voyeurs, the grubs and slugs and drones, the curious, me and you. Blue-blood dandies and Dun and Bradstreet–adored dudes screamed for see-and-be-seen tables, but Elaine kept them iced at the bar—a gorgon guarding those sexy front stations for her boys.

No need to call one's agent or one's broker or one's bookie or one's wife's divorce lawyer to find out one's worth. One had only to stand at Elaine's bar with a watch, waiting for a table, smiling big, as if the telltale drag on the minute hand weren't all that painful. As if a wave to the back room weren't really fatal. The night everyone's memories fondle gleefully: Henry Ford and the dazzling Cristina cooling at the bar, then exiled to the Ragu room, Elaine's Siberia. If you are only a simple, insecure scrivener with typewriter ink on your fingers, who else in this town pampers you at the expense of a topline Ford? "She's just a middle-class Italian," says Elaine.

Divorces were crueler because of Elaine's. If the screenwriter Eleanor Perry was appalled realizing she'd spent the last six years of her marriage six nights a week at Elaine's, it was the marriage, not Elaine's, that appalled her. In a moment of mock tragedy after splitting from Dan Greenburg, Nora Ephron lamented, "Do you think Dan gets Elaine's in the separation agreement?"

Elaine's is a cabaret. Bobby Zarem is keeping Richard Harris eloquent and civilized on beer until Elaine insists Harris have a "real drink." Suddenly Harris is storming a stranger at the bar. "People go hoping to see Robert Frost in his cups or Solzhenitsyn decked by Kurt Vonnegut or Norman Mailer in a violent Maileresque moment," David Halberstam observes. But Elaine's true pets are not instantly recognizable. I'm not sure I could pick Bruce Jay Friedman out of a lineup. Not even Elaine recognizes Antonioni. Sticks him in the back room. In town to promote his book on Chicago's Mayor Daley, Mike Royko is a disappointed tourist. "Elaine's," he says. "The food was awful. It was crowded. We were rushed. I spent the whole time twisting my neck around to see everyone else twisting their necks around." Next time Royko comes with Jimmy Breslin, John Lindsay, Jules Feiffer. He doesn't have to twist his neck. "By the end of the evening I was threatening to elope with Elaine, and my wife was upset because she found two guys making love in the ladies' room."

Moving traffic, guarding the big "training table" for her boys, freighting the nobodies in and out, bouncing drunks, and shouting down sassers, Elaine can be outrageous. One night, she has just seated two Englishmen after an interminable wait when Gay and Nan Talese walk in with Teresa Wright. "It's already been such an awful night for you, you

Writer Gay Talese
and his wife, Nan
Talese, who has
her own imprint at
Doubleday

won't be surprised if I move you to another table," she says, jollying the men toward the rear to clear a choice station for Gay. "I don't have a table free for you," Elaine tells the late playwright Muriel Resnik and the author Victor Jackson another evening. "But you know these people. I'll put you with them." A few minutes later, she informs the original occupants of the table, "Come with me, I have a table for you back here." Muriel's mouth drops. "I'm not saying a word. She terrifies me," whispers the about to be displaced woman.

Since I was a kid I've always been good with people. I understand what people are talking about. A lot of times, there's a writer coming in for dinner, he's been working all day, maybe all evening long, and he's decided he has to get out of the house. He comes in and sits down, and he's talking from his mouth, but his mind is still back where he was. And it's the oddest thing to see. You can't even interfere with it. He's disconnected from who he is. But he knew he had to stop. I was at a Yankee ballgame, sitting in Steinbrenner's box, next to Nan Talese, who has her own imprint at Doubleday. She got to talking about somebody's book she was editing and said she was beginning to think the author would never finish it. He's holding on to it, afraid to let it go. I said, "From my experience, you've got to help him. Is there a point where you feel the book has an ending?" Nan said she thought she knew where that was. I said, "Well, okay, help him. If he wants to write another book after that, he can take it from there." And she did. But what was funny that day at the ballgame was that the agent Swifty Lazar was sitting on the other side of the partition between the boxes, and, overhearing us, he suddenly popped up and said, "I'll do the movie deal for you."

—ELAINE

"The photographer Jonathan Becker had taken me to see the master photographer Brassai's show at the Marlboro Gallery in 1979. We asked Brassai if he would like to come for dinner, thinking all the time that he would be booked, since he's such an incredible world-famous artist. But nobody had asked him. I was really appalled. So he and his wife turned up on a Saturday night. Plimpton was there and I said, 'George, it's my party but invite him to your table. I think it will make him feel better because you know who he is and it would be interesting.' We had a big dinner. Lots of wine. Then he asked if we could get the *Times*. We got the *Times* and there was a double-page review of his work. Well, he was just so elated. We broke open a bottle of his favorite Champagne, Laurent-Perrier, and toasted him. It turned out that it was his eightieth birthday. "

—ELAINE

Everyone Comes to Elaine's

13

Brassai and a slim Elaine in the 1970s

PHOTOGRAPH BY JONATHAN BECKER

After years of being surrounded by gorgeous women," Elaine says, "lookers who take tremendous care of themselves, I guess it finally got to me—a fat lady in a muu-muu surrounded by size sixes in designer clothes. So when my joint really got going, I mean *really* got going, that's when I said to myself, Elaine, it's time you got going, get yourself in a shape you can go into Bergdorf and buy a dress, a really honest-to-God dress, not this shmatte that hangs on you like a fucking tent.

"I had tried everything under the sun—Hindu diets, depressants, hypnosis. I went to Dr. Herb Siegel, who hypnotized me and implanted suggestions that were supposed to change my thought process and attitude toward eating. I really wanted to cooperate, wanted to suppress the eating thing, but my childhood background was just too strong—being force-fed by my mother, having to eat to please her. The hypnosis didn't work because you may emotionally on one level want to change your eating habits, your desires, but there's something else in you from way back that's stronger.

"So now, at three hundred and fifty-six pounds, the time had come to stop kidding myself and bite the bullet. I checked myself into St. Luke's Hospital weight control unit and for months I stuck with the diet and the exercises and the fucking yoga, sessions with the diet shrink who kept telling me to think thin, and as the mounds of weight melted away, the surgeons stitching up my skin, I can tell you getting on that scale every day was an absolute high, to see that needle drop, drop, drop—all the way down to a hundred and forty-six—two hundred and ten pounds melted away, and on the day I walked out of St. Luke's I went straight to Bergdorf's and bought a gorgeous Donna Karan that had a belt around the waist—

So now, at three hundred and fifty-six pounds, the time had come to stop kidding myself and bite the bullet.

Chris Noth and Jill Hennessy

PHOTOGRAPH BY JESSICA BURSTEIN

When I was copious, I didn't feel I was accepted socially which makes you defensive—or, as Liz Smith said in her column, "bellicose."

Elaine Kaufman had a waist! And a belt with notches! Then I had my knees fixed—they were busted from carrying all that weight my whole life—and I got new glasses, fixed my teeth, restyled my hair, and best of all, I found myself singing in the shower! What you probably don't realize is that obese people don't sing in the shower because while you're passing the soap over your body, that's nothing to sing about. But now with my St. Luke's body I am all of a sudden singing in the shower.

"When I was copious, I didn't feel I was accepted socially, which makes you defensive—or, as Liz Smith said in her column, 'bellicose': You don't accept me, I don't accept you. But when you go from heavy to svelte, you don't know how to handle svelte and you become vulnerable. I'd never been vulnerable before—all my life, defensive, but now I'm happy with what I see in the mirror . . . but something's missing—a big something—a man: What good's all this if you haven't got a man to appreciate it, and not just a man . . . but a husband? I always pooh-poohed marriage—not for me—being married was so locked up. I always wanted to come and go as I pleased. But now, the way I look—I'm yearning. I can't believe it. Yearning! Gertrude Niessen has a Broadway song I used to imitate—one of those second acts I crashed . . . very apropos . . .

> *I wanna get married*
> *I wanna get spliced*
> *I long to be knotted and see my friends potted*
> *I wanna be confettied and riced . . .*

"I'd go into my place at night in one of my new Bergdorf dresses, with my new Kenneth Lane jewelry, doused with sensuous Obsession perfume, walking on rose petals, except . . . for one thing—now that I was beautiful, I wanted to get hooked up. But you know the saying: Be careful what you wish for because you may get it."

Tommy Carney, Elaine's bartender for the past twenty years, says, "Elaine looked like a million bucks. She had a whole new wardrobe and she was feeling like a teenager. One night, in comes a guy, been in a couple of times before, Henry Ball, I knew him from 1958 working with him at the Four Seasons restaurant. I was a waiter; he was a captain. He's a Brit with a Liverpool accent, resembled the English actor Bob Hoskins, kind of a cross between Michael Caine and Mick Jagger. He was an okay guy when I knew him, real straight dude, but for twenty-five years I haven't seen this guy. He orders a Perrier and tells me he's the new food and beverage director at the Helmsley Palace, which just opened. He says he would like to meet Elaine, who's down at the end of the bar, toting up checks."

"I go down the bar to where he's sitting," Elaine says, "and I say to him, 'Tommy tells me you're at the Helmsley Palace.'

"'Well, yeah,' he says, 'I'm the new food and beverage director.'

"'I've noticed you at the bar a couple of times—one Perrier and you skedaddle.'

"'I come up on my breaks.'

"'What's so great about my Perrier?'

"'Not for the Perrier. For you.'

"'Aw, come on,' I say.

"'To be specific,' he says, 'for your eyes.'

"'My what?'

"'Do you know, Elaine, you have the most remarkable eyes—they have a softness, a luminosity, the way they regard people, the way they glow with love for your favorites, and the way they dance when you laugh, and how they snap cold when you're angry.'

"'My eyes? I wear glasses.'

"'They frame those eyes, like the frame on a Rembrandt or a Renoir.'

"'They're just . . . eyes.'

"'Elaine, the eyes are the windows of the soul. You can look in a person's eyes and see her soul. Especially when you're up close to her like this . . . I've thought about you a lot, Elaine. How you are here every night making all these people happy, but who's making you happy when you close up at night to go home . . . alone? And in the morning, no one to share your coffeepot. I know how it is. Your eyes tell me how lonely, how unfulfilled you are. You know what Saint Jerome said? 'The face is the mirror of the mind, and eyes, without speaking, confess the secrets of the heart.'

"'Saint Jerome?'

"'Eyes, without speaking, confess the secrets of the heart.'

"'They do?'

"His face is close to mine as he looks smack into my eyes. Like I said, being svelte, my defenses are down—way down.

"'And what *your* eyes confess,' he says, 'is that your heart's secret is that you are hungry to be loved.'

"'And you can see that?'

"'In your eyes.'

"'Really?'

"'You would be easy to love, Elaine.'

"Before I know what the hell I'm doing, this Henry guy is

But this now svelte person for the first time since she can remember, she is Ginger Rogers shaking her ass in the arms of Henry Ball.

PHOTOGRAPH BY JESSICA BURSTEIN

kissing me right at my own bar—like some of the three A.M. characters I boot outa here—twenty minutes after the hello he's got his
tongue in my mouth. Well. . . look, I wished for a man, I got a man.
He came in every night after that for a week, took me out after
midnight, and we'd go dancing at one of the clubs. The fact is, just
as they don't sing in the shower, fat people don't dance because of
the trouble they'd have moving three hundred and fifty-six
pounds doing the tango. But this now svelte person for the first
time since she can remember, she is Ginger Rogers shaking her ass
in the arms of Henry Ball. And just as he had put his lips on mine
twenty minutes after he met me, now, one week after that

Tommy Carney,
patriarch of the
Elaine's bar

shmiekaly smooch, while Henry's gliding me around the dance floor, he's got his lips at my ear, whispering . . .

"'Elaine?'

"'Yes?'

"'Elaine?'

"'Yeah?'

"'Will you marry me?'

"'Will I?. . .What! . . .One week—Henry, I know you one week and you're asking me to marry you?'

"'One week, one year, does time matter? Our souls are already married, aren't they?'

"'But *one week* . . .'

"'We met long ago in Thebes on the Nile . . .'

"'Henry, stop—I'm going to faint.'

"'It's been a long voyage but we have finally arrived at our destination.'

"'No, no . . . not yet.'

"'Mrs. Henry Ball has a nice ring to it . . . and one around your finger.'

"That was it—one week—Saint Jerome and Elaine Kaufman—go figure.

W*e set the wedding for Christmas week and I'm* busy making all the plans and arrangements for Elaine Kaufman, the bride . . . but then came that Sunday—that fucking Sunday, just before Christmas. We were doing a party for the cast of *Forty-second Street*, David Merrick and Gower Champion's production. We're playing the score, the chorus kids are grooving, and everybody's having a helluva time, including the future Mrs. Ball in her swishy Bergdorf finery, when one of the waiters comes to get me to answer the phone. I have to yell over the noise. The voice says, Is this Elaine Kaufman? Yes. This is the manager of the Helmsley Palace. One of our employees, Henry Ball, has given us your name as someone who might come to help him.

"I grab my coat, latch on to one of the limos at the curb. Two guys meet me in the Helmsley lobby and I'm taken down to the basement and into the wine cellar, where, on the floor, with several empty wine bottles strewn around him, is my husband-to-be plastered to the gills. He's had a go at some of the best wines on their shelves. He slobbers when he tries to talk and he's got spaghetti for legs. A couple of Helmsley people help me get him into a taxi, sort of stuff him in, and we come back here. I leave Henry in the taxi while I get Tommy the barman. We go a few blocks and get off at Dorian's Red Hand. Luckily there are no customers. Tommy and I prop him up at the bar and order coffee. Tommy says, 'Since when did you become a boozer?' And Henry says, 'Go fuck yourself.' Tommy says, 'When I knew you, you were an okay guy. Now look at you—a drunken turd.' Whereupon Henry throws a roundhouse punch at Tommy that barely misses, and Tommy jumps up and wallops Henry into the bar. I'm screaming, No! No! Stop it! Stop it! The Dorian's bartender is trying to help when Henry picks up a chair and throws it at Tommy, who ducks the chair and belts Henry with another punch. The cops are there in a flash and we get the hell out of there, propping up Henry between us.

"The next day, Henry is all over me and Tommy, full of apology, mea culpa, all that crap. 'Elaine, sweetheart, I'm sorry as hell, sorry, rotten thing, but listen, a man's allowed one misstep, isn't he? Just the once. Don't know why it happened but it won't happen again.

He's had a go at some of the best wines on their shelves. He slobbers when he tries to talk and he's got spaghetti for legs.

Ever. I promise. Please, I'm me, look at me, I'm me—that other guy, last night, I won't let him in again, not ever. I promise. Okay? You got my word of honor.'

"So from then on, every night he's in the restaurant, behaving himself, sitting at a back table smoking my best cigars and drinking the oldest port—well, actually, not drinking it but dipping the end of his cigar in it.

"The wedding's a week away and I'm getting a lot of push not to marry Henry. His ex-wife called to warn me about him, but I just thought, Oh, hell, a disgruntled woman trying to get back at him. Tommy, and several Irish and English people who knew him, all after me to write him off as a nasty piece of work, but, what you gotta understand, I'm in love with the guy, I really am, or at least I'm in love with getting married, and there's no sign of his getting out of control again. Besides, I thought I could turn him around, that things would work out—all those fucking clichés.

So just before Christmas Day, we get all dressed up and go down to City Hall. Mayor David Dinkins is there to officiate, but all the regulars were back at the restaurant waiting for us. Joe Salamone and Carlo, one of my waiters, had made a giant baked Alaska and put it in the freezer downstairs, but when time came to bring it up, it was too big to get it through the freezer door. So Joe has to go out and get an electric saw to cut it in half. As they're bringing it up, it topples over on Carlo and he's covered with whipped cream from head to toe. But finally they get it up, and put it on Woody Allen's table and replace all the whipped cream. It's enormous, the size of that tabletop. Carlo gets a bottle of Bacardi One-Fifty-One and as I in my new size-ten frock and Henry come into the restaurant, Carlo douses the cake with the entire bottle, puts a match to it as everyone sings 'Here Comes the Bride,' and someone's playing the piano when ga-boom! The baked Alaska explodes and burns, sending clouds of black smoke all over the place with all of us getting the hell out of there, so instead of being confettied and riced, my wedding reception is out on the sidewalk in front of my restaurant holding plates of burned Alaska. As it turned out, the reception for the bride and groom was a fit beginning for the marriage.

"For our honeymoon, we went to the Super Bowl in New Orleans. Henry knew a whole bunch of jazz people who lived there and we went to a lot of parties. But I'm having a tough time with Henry on the eating thing. Every time we had a meal he kept saying, 'Oh, you've got to have this, at least have a taste,' and I would say I can't eat that, it will make me heavy again, I've got to be really careful. 'Oh, just a taste of this, a taste of that,' he kept pushing this food at me, knowing what it would do to me, and I was a mess. I was in such conflict, because on the one hand I was trying to hold myself, and on the other hand I liked the guy and wanted to please him by eating, just the way I had tried to please my mother way back when. In no time at all, all that hard work I had done at the hospital, all the hard work to keep myself svelte, was for nothing and the needle on the scale went up a lot faster than when it came down.

"We went to Liverpool for me to meet his family. It's his mother's birthday, a little family party, and when I went to get a cake, he said, No cake! But I got one anyway.

"Then, while we're having drinks and eating the cake, he suddenly turns on his brother and starts to beat the shit out of him, and if that's not enough, he goes after his sister and beats her up too, slams them around. I've seen a lot of fistfights and stuff in my joint

I'm having a tough time with Henry on the eating thing. Every time we had a meal he kept saying, "Oh, you've got to have this, at least have a taste."

Writer Jerzy Kosinski in the good days before his suicide

but I never saw anything like this in my life. But I knew to stay calm. When you're going against somebody in a tirade, you better stay calm until he passes through it. If you go head-to-head with him, he'll kill you. I guess I had wanted to get married so badly that I had ignored all the signs, or pretended I didn't see them.

"Of course, afterward, when we got back to the States, it was the same old I'm sorry—I'll be different, I'll be different, please give me another chance, I promise you, I'll be different—but now I knew he couldn't change and I was on guard. He tried to get in on the running of the restaurant but I stiff-armed him on that."

"He had a go at me many a time," Tommy says, "and I'd tell him, 'If you want to come over this fucking bar, you come, and you make one move, pal, and you're going to be dead. Put a hand on that cash register and I'm going to kill you.'"

"I went home one night," Elaine says, "and Henry had a bunch of people there, and they were drinking and what not—it was all very sloppy. I eased them out of there. We're alone then and Henry's in a drunken rage.

"'You bitch! Breaking up my party! How the hell you got the right to come in here and throw your big-ass weight around!'

"'Henry,' I say, 'it's time we got things straight. I just can't have you in the restaurant anymore. You get drunk and I'm told you beat up one of my customers in the men's room over something that was nothing. And you've been giving Tommy a hard time at the bar, bullying him to give you cash out of the register. I've had it up to here with you—now stay the hell out of my place. I don't want to see you in there again.'

"Henry pulls a knife out of his pocket, grabs me around the neck with one arm, and puts the blade to my throat. He's scream-

I've seen a lot of fistfights and stuff in my joint but I never saw anything like this in my life.

He passes out. I pick up the knife and get to the phone and call a lawyer friend who tells me to quickly get out of the apartment.

ing at me. 'Your place, huh? Your fuckin' place! Well, I've got news for you—I'm the husband, I got rights—you tellin' me to stay out, fuck you, and fuck that Tommy bastard, I'm the husband, I've got my rights, I'm comin' in whenever I want and I'm drinkin' what I want to drink and I'm getting' cash whenever I need it, you hear?' He is pressing on the blade, but I'm being absolutely still even though he's cutting me a little. 'You hear? You hear? Or else this knife'll go a little deeper . . . see, like this, but deeper, deeper, and you know what? Your whole goddamn restaurant will be all mine.' The booze is starting to get to him and he is sagging . . .'Your fat ass'll be six feet under . . . and I'll be the main man . . . I know restaurants.' He is wobbly now and he lowers the knife, I don't move a muscle. He's passing out. 'The Four Seasons . . . the Four Seasons, not your dump . . . I had my station, six tables . . . Captain Ball . . . ' He sags to the floor and drops the knife. 'That fuckin' Tommy, one of my waiters . . . big man now behind the bar . . . I was his boss . . . Hear that? Captain Ball . . . I could've been maitre d' . . . except for . . . I mean that one time . . . goddamnit . . . I could've been maitre d'. . . You hear? I could've worn the white tie . . . stood at the entrance . . . oh, yeah . . . I could've worn . . . the white . . . tie . . .' He passes out. I pick up the knife and get to the phone and call a lawyer friend who tells me to quickly get out of the apartment, and as soon as Henry leaves, to go back with a bodyguard and have the locks changed. Next day, Henry came begging at the door. Same old crap.

"'Please, Elaine, please, I'm so damn sorry, I don't know what got into me. I love you, really, really love you, and I'm so goddamn sorry, really I am, sincerely.'

"'Well, so am I, Henry,' I say, 'sorry that I've been a fool to get involved with you, sorry that I've lost my svelte, sorry that the bubble has popped in my face. Get the hell out of my life, Henry—those windows to my heart are shut.'

"I hired security men to keep him out of the restaurant and paid him a thousand dollars to get a divorce. He eventually went back to Liverpool, where he died, boozed and drugged, about six, seven years ago. The night I heard about it, I opened a bottle of Cristal Champagne, not to celebrate his passing, miserable bastard though he was, but to toast whoever it is who looks after me . . . obviously, not Saint Jerome."

I *suppose it was bound to happen.*
Assuming, of course, that the event itself was feasible. Therefore, when it actually did occur (a little after one in the morning, November 5, 1967), I was not all that surprised. Indeed, I remember thinking, soon after realizing just what was going on, I have been expecting this; now I know why I've been coming to Elaine's all these years.

That it was in fact occurring was beyond dispute—Mailer saw it, Buzz Farber, Bruce, Billy Friedkin, Richardson, at the next table Mstislav Rostropovich, André Previn, farther to the front Andy Warhol, the socialite Dee-Dee Ryan, Rudolf Nureyev, God knows who else in the back. And, of course, Elaine. It was Elaine who opened the door.

There'd been a fight at the bar. I can't remember over what. Buzz had tried to step in, but Elaine had said no, she'd handle it, and she did. None of us had ever seen the guy before. He was huge, a neck as big as his shoulders. Elaine picked him right off the stool. She said, "We don't want your sort here," and out he went.

The light came first.

She'd kicked the door open, keeping it open with her foot for the old heave-ho. The light came in as the guy was going out.

The next thing I remember was a sense of . . . I guess "presence." I mean, one could somehow feel Him in the room before He could be seen.

Elaine had shut the door, thinking the glow nothing but the glare of a headlight. Then she realized who it was standing next to her. He said, "I've heard about your place."

She led Him to the back, to a quiet spot. He said He'd like to be alone. He didn't want to impose, He said.

It was hard not to ogle. But of course no one did. Elaine came back and said He seemed just like a regular guy, no airs.

We asked what He'd ordered, and she said veal parmigiana, well done, which we all thought was odd, but who could say. And then He came over—or rather, suddenly He was there. He looked down on all of us; we were at the Big Table. He said, "Is this the Big Table? The one I've been hearing so much about?" Richardson asked if He'd like to sit down, and He did. Whereupon He turned to Mailer and said, "They tell me you think you're tough." Norman fainted.

Well, we were staggered.

"He'll be all right," He said. "Not to worry." Then He thanked Elaine for allowing Him in without a reservation, and left. He did not pay His bill, and Elaine said she thought He just didn't understand how things were done. Then Elaine bought everybody drinks. Then Norman bought everybody drinks; then Richardson, then I, then Elaine again. By and by, one by one, we staggered out, agreeing, as we did, that it had definitely been an amazing night. But then, in those days it was that kind of place.

—ARTHUR KOPIT, *playwright*

" Mike Nichols was shooting scenes for *Heartburn* in the vicinity of the restaurant, which was open for lunch in those days. One day Mike came in with Jack Nicholson for a late lunch. They looked around and Mike said, 'You're not very busy, are you Elaine?' And I said, 'Yeah, well I've been to some of your movies in the afternoon.' *"*

—ELAINE

Everyone Comes to Elaine's

14

Jack Nicholson and Elaine
at a Knicks game

Elaine shook off her marriage debacle, water off a duck's back, and in no way did it affect the person she was and always would be. Big-time saloon keepers all had distinctive signatures and Elaine is no exception. Texas Guinan's greeting was "Hello, suckers!" Toots Shor would welcome his notables with "Hiya, you lousy crum-bum!" Danny Lavezzo of PJ Clarke's held court in a quiet alcove near the entrance to the dining room where he would receive all comers; Sherman Billingsley would personally unhook the velvet cord at the door for those who were special; when an established regular would pony up to the bar, Tim Costello's inevitable query was "What'll it be—the same old rotgut?" and Elaine's signature greeting has four stages depending on the seeding of the arriver: stage one (newcomers), a nod of the head; stage two (semiregulars), a handshake; stage three (regulars), a peck on the cheek; stage four (the favored few), a stand-up kiss and hug.

Sometimes her favored few come in for rather peculiar visits to the Second Avenue shrine. There was an Easter when the actor Michael J. Pollard came in with his parents. "I waited on them myself," Elaine says. 'So what'll you have?' I asked. 'Nothing,' they said. 'We've just come to watch Michael eat.' And that's what they did. Michael had soup and Jack Daniel's, and they watched. Milanese and Jack Daniel's. And they watched. I was too overcome to say anything."

Elaine had a similar experience on a Mother's Day, when Charles Nelson Reilly booked a table for dinner with his mother, whom he was meeting at the train. "Charles had made money for the first time in *Bye Bye Birdie*," Elaine says, "and he wanted to give Mom a very nice dinner. So when the menus arrived, he says,

"I waited on them myself. So what'll you have?" I asked. "Nothing," they said. "We've just come to watch Michael eat."

'C'mon, Mom, order, I've got money now, we're okay.' And she says, 'I'd like a cheese sandwich.' He says, 'Have something else! Please!' But that's all she wanted. Poor Charles was so destroyed. But then he tried to do something nice for his father who didn't have any teeth. So with his newfound money Charles bought his father a set of choppers. The next thing Charles knew, his father, now resplendent with his new teeth, split from his mother for greener pastures."

A certain snobby, lockjaw Long Island set used to dine at a society restaurant called Mortimer's but on this particular night several of them began showing up for a table they had reserved at Elaine's.

Writer Dan Jenkins and his wife, June

As the first couple passed by, Elaine wondered if Mortimer's was closed. Several more arrived, and one of them greeted Elaine: "Are you going to ski this year, Elaine?" "No," Elaine answered, "Jews don't ski."

There are people who can't wait to get there with their friends so that their friends can see them say hello to Elaine and her say hello to them.

Joe Allen, who now has eight restaurants around the world, says that "Elaine could have done what I did and probably done it better, but she never attempted a second place. She could really have done whatever she wanted to do. But that's her approach and it certainly works. It's like every night is New Year's Eve at Elaine's. There are very few of these places anymore, if any. There are people who can't wait to get there with their friends so that their friends can see them say hello to Elaine and her say hello to them. I would say that by almost any measure, in terms of longevity, in terms of heat, for lack of a better word, it's the most enduring place in New York. Now, anyway. And certainly one of the most enduring places ever. By virtue of its location and its low-keyness, it being way up off the beaten track, that distinguishes it. To go all the way up to Eighty-eighth and Second, you are among the converted."

One of the converted, a recipient of Elaine's top accolade, the hug, is the wonderful humorist Dan Jenkins: "It was a day like any other day. I woke up in the late afternoon with a hangover that would flatten David Rockefeller's bank account. I crawled out of bed, gargled with some J&B, and drew myself a warm tub of Visine. Feeling better later on, I dug out my cleanest pair of wrinkled corduroys, slipped into my Royal Sydney Golf Club windbreaker, and headed out the door for Elaine's. I was calling on another plate of four-hundred-dollar pasta.

Andy Warhol

"As I rounded the corner of Eighty-eighth and Second, I could already hear Larry L. King's voice from inside the restaurant. He was yelling about tax shelters and hunchbacked dwarf editors. I knew I was home.

"Somehow, the place looked different inside. The front room was larger, and there were a lot of guys there from the Polo Lounge. I glanced at the back room to see who had been deported. It was redecorated with ICM filing cabinets.

"'What year is it?' I asked Elaine unsteadily, staring at the half dozen World Series rings that dangled around her neck.

"She said, 'Where have you been?'

"'I don't know,' I said in a weary voice. 'The last thing I remember was Sophie's flashback to Auschwitz.'

"Elaine seated me at the table in the front room that had become mine after Noël Coward died. A waiter came over and began to recite the evening's squid specials. Interrupting him, I said I would just have the epaulet soup, please, with a side order of Sam Cohen's unlisted phone numbers. Things had gradually changed in Elaine's since the days when Jack Richardson wore a black cape and did card tricks in the corner, when everyone else thought a poker game was going on.

"In those days, a man talked about the pieces he had written about Long Island potato farmers and how it looked as if they were about to wind up in a hardcover collection for Little, Brown. Now a man talked about his share of the producer's gross after two-point-seven times negative.

"The sportswriter Mike Lupica came in from a screening and said he might have been hasty in discarding Sigourney Weaver so quickly in favor of Debra Winger. Roy Blount came in and doodled

I said I would just have the epaulet soup, please, with a side order of Sam Cohen's unlisted phone numbers.

on the tablecloth, writing a love song about okra. Bruce Friedman came in with his head bandaged and his carriage return in a sling. He said he had just read where Saul Bellow felt American writers weren't trying hard enough. Bud Shrake called long-distance from the Westwood Marquis to say that his script was still in intensive care, and it was touch-and-go whether it would survive all the attacks of motivation.

"Presently, twenty Texans were at my table, the same ones who were usually responsible for the pasta costing four hundred dollars. Elaine sat down with us and fondly remembered the summer night in '67 when a Texas visitor actually paid for dinner.

"Eventually, one of my guests asked Elaine the direction to the men's room. Elaine happened to be in the middle of a story about a fashion lady with a three-foot handshake. She gestured toward the rear of the room and said, 'Uh . . . go to Michael Caine and take a right!'

"With that, Elaine stood up to greet a good friend who had entered, a friend who wasn't a celebrity. Elaine didn't realize she had left us with what would have to be the title to any autobiography she might one day attempt to write: *Go to Michael Caine and Take a Right!*

"Her lines have always been as good as her veal chops or set decoration, and it is for all of this that we keep going back. I think. Well, that and picking up the mail."

Reflections on Thirty Years of Ordering from the Same Menu at Least Once a Week

Pasta?
Basta.
Scungilli?
Not really.
Calamari?
I'm sorry.
Espresso?
I guesso.

—Peter Stone

A t Elaine's, the unexpected is expected, like the night Imelda Marcos made a reservation. In advance of her arrival, a van pulled up and six sharpshooters armed with weapons emerged and stationed themselves on rooftops, across from the restaurant and on top of the restaurant. A short time later, a second van disgorged four bodyguards who, with their armpits bulging, came into Elaine's and occupied tables in the corners. Then came the limo with Imelda herself, all decked out in her Filipino finery, acting queenly, but it turned out okay; she had a good time because Andy Warhol was there that night and Imelda owned one of his Marilyn Monroes—the one with six green faces. Imelda introduced herself to Warhol, sat down at his table, and suggested that perhaps he'd like to do the same thing with her face. Andy was polite but he didn't jump at the opportunity. It is rather chilling to imagine six green Imeldas staring at you from your dining room wall.

I told Michael, the maitred', "If I come in with a date and look like I'm having a terrible time, get me out quick."

Many romantic liaisons have been forged at Elaine's. The writer-producer David Black says, "After my divorce, I told Michael, the maitre d', 'If I come in with a date and look like I'm having a terrible time, get me out quick.'

"'What if you look like you're having a wonderful time?' Michael asked.

"'Get me out quicker!'

"For a month or two this system worked fine, but the first time I brought Barbara to Elaine's, Michael misunderstood and tried to hustle us out. But this wasn't a quick score. This was love. I kept delaying. Michael, not getting it, kept trying to move things along, shoving the check under my nose, clearing the table.

"The photographer Jessica Burstein happened to be there that night and she took a picture of Barbara and me kissing, which ended up in *New York* magazine—which is how Barbara's relatives found out we were serious.

"And we were serious. We asked Elaine if we could get married in the restaurant. Elaine said yes. I explained I was thinking of a few close friends, a couple of drinks, nothing fancy.

"Elaine turned to Barbara and asked, 'This your first wedding?'

"Barbara said, 'Yes.'

"Elaine hit me upside the head and said, 'What'sa matter with you? Do it right!'

"And Elaine helped us do it right: a hundred guests, garlands around the canopy poles outside a chuppah at the back of the restaurant, even mashed potatoes made with gribenes—onions fried with chicken fat—although when, a few months later, I asked the chef, Barry, to again make some gribenes for dinner, he refused. 'Don't you know,' he said, 'that gribenes have killed more Jews than the Holocaust?'"

"I went to David and Barbara's wedding at Elaine's," Tom Fontana says. "The restaurant magically became a synagogue / chapel, not so much because of the decorations but because of the spirit of love and friendship which Elaine created that day."

Nora Ephron and Nick Pileggi, who wrote *Goodfellas*, began their relationship at Elaine's. "I didn't meet Nick at Elaine's," Nora says, "I'd known him for years, and in fact, back in the seventies I'd had dinner at Elaine's with him and his then-wife. But one night in 1983, when I was between things, I went to Elaine's with Alice and Michael Arlen, the author. Nick had seen me there a week earlier, and had figured out I was probably up for grabs. He came over to the Arlens' table and asked me for my phone number, and that was pretty much that. So I finally married the right person thanks to Elaine's, or some such.

"A couple of years after Nick and I got together Elaine had

some sort of big party celebrating something like her twentieth or twenty-fifth year of being in business, and I remember realizing that for most of us in the room, it was the true college reunion—it was the place where we'd grown up, lived part of our lives, survived our divorces, taken a bow or two on the occasion of a well-turned sentence, and gone from being almost writers to being writers, or something of the sort. I think it was my friend Alice Arlen who once said that just being there was a kind of validation."

There was the night that Mia Farrow asked Michael Caine to introduce her to Woody Allen with whom she subsequently cohabitated with less than satisfactory results.

There were other notable romantic beginnings. In the late sixties, Judy Garland was at a rear table celebrating the newly formed alliance between her young accompanist and music composer, Peter Allen, and her daughter Liza.

Also, as previously noted, there was the night that Mia Farrow asked Michael Caine to introduce her to Woody Allen with whom she subsequently cohabited with less than satisfactory results.

It should be pointed out that there have also been liaisons of a different nature. Bob Drury says, "I'd once witnessed the former New York Mets first baseman Keith Hernandez captured in flagrante delicto in the bathroom with the date of the Manhattan socialite and gadabout Gianni Uzielli. 'Johnny' was a descendant of the Rothschilds, the son of the Italian ambassador to the United Nations, a good guy who was once married to the heiress Anne Ford. He said he learned of their divorce when his Park Avenue doorman told him one night, 'You don't live here anymore!' Anyway, he'd come in late with a comely companion and plopped down at a table with Elaine and Hernandez. Hernandez excused himself to head for the loo. Gianni's date followed. An indecorous amount of time elapsed, and Gianni finally wandered back to the restrooms. Then the whole bar heard his scream: 'You whore!' This was followed by a flustered Hernandez grabbing his coat, saying good night to Elaine, and vanishing. On his heels was Gianni's equally crimson-checked date. The two were barely out the door before Gianni took his seat, straightened his Turnbull and Asser tie, and, in a gesture dripping with aplomb, bought the house a round."

PHOTOGRAPH BY JESSICA BURSTEIN

New York Mets legend Keith Hernandez

"We have a lot of very young people coming in today. It's amusing when they ask about one of the photographs that Richard Avedon gave me, a large framed blowup that I have on the wall, of Dwight Eisenhower and Humphrey Bogart, side by side. They can mostly figure out who Bogart is, but they have trouble with Eisenhower. They ask me, 'Who's the guy next to Bogart?'"

—ELAINE

Everyone Comes to Elaine's

15

Saturday Night Live castmembers—
Chevy Chase, Dan Aykroyd,
and John Belushi—with producer
Lorne Michaels in the Elaine's kitchen

PHOTOGRAPH BY JONATHAN BECKER

*O*n a couple of occasions, the indigenous commotion at Elaine's has been enhanced by armed stickups. The first intrusion occurred after closing hours when the bartender left the front door unlocked while he went to see a friend parked at the curb across the street. In comes a little guy in a long white coat brandishing a large revolver.

"He grabbed me," Elaine recalls, "threw me around while he's yelling this is a holdup, as if that hadn't occurred to me. He orders me into the men's room but I come back out and watch what's happening. The bartender returns and the robber puts the gun to his head and demands he fill a bag with all the money. The bartender, a hot-blooded Armenian, says, 'You're making me nervous,' and he pushes the gun away. But he empties the cash register into a bag and the robber takes off.

"The cops nab him pretty quickly. They go up to Harlem, looking for a little guy in a long white leather coat—turns out he just got out of jail and they put him right back in.

"The second holdup was a bigger deal. It's at the busiest time of the night. The place is packed. Frank Waters, who was once a detective, is my bartender. Two guys come in, one tall and porky, the other short and skinny, they sit at the bar, order drinks. Frank comes over to me and says he thinks these guys are jailbirds. I ask him why he thinks that. He says the way they ordered the drinks, like they hadn't been in a bar for a long time. I think they asked for 'highballs.' Frank thinks they're loaded and casing us for a stickup. We had a buzzer under the counter at the end of the bar that hooked into the security company, but Frank said we better not use it because if we press the alarm they're going to come in with the

He grabbed me, threw me around while he's yelling this is a holdup, as if that hadn't occurred to me.

Sopranos star James Gandolfini

PHOTOGRAPH BY JESSICA BURSTEIN

guns up and if these guys have guns, there's going to be a gun battle. So I said, What'll we do? He said I've got to get rid of everyone
at the bar. So while these two guys went to the men's room, Frank
got everyone to clear out.

"These guys come back to the bar. I pretend I'm reading the
newspaper when the big one sticks a gun into me but I just keep
reading. What am I going to do? I don't think screaming's going to
help. Anyway, I'm not good at that. He says, 'Just keep reading the
paper, you'll be okay.' He makes a pouch out of his jacket and starts
putting money from the cash register into it.

*He has a gun on
them and tells
them to lie
facedown on the
floor and give
him their wallets
and rings and
watches.*

"Meanwhile, the little guy has herded up all the waiters in the
back near the bread drawer where they can't be seen by people in
the restaurant. He has a gun on them and tells them to lie facedown
on the floor and give him their wallets and rings and watches. So
they all do that but when the robber makes a count he sees he's
missing a wallet and gets very agitated. He demands, 'Who's holding out? I'm gonna blow him away!' One of the waiters, Nicola,
says, 'Don't shoot me. Here's my wallet. Shoot this guy,' pointing
to a fellow waiter, 'he doesn't have any kids. I've got a kid.' The
robber puts the gun to Nicola's head but doesn't pull the trigger.

"The little robber comes back to the bar and I can see he's very
agitated to the point that he looks ready to shoot up the place. But
the other one tells him to cool it, they've got the loot, so they go
out and grab a cab. What I found out is that they went a few blocks
down Second Avenue, where they stopped at a liquor store that
they held up. The woman who owned it was upstairs making dinner for her daughter and son-in-law who were minding the store.
The robbers point their guns and tell the customers and the daughter and son-in-law to hand over their money. Everybody does,

except the son-in-law holds back some of the cash and the little robber point-blank blows him away. Shows you how lucky Nicola was.

"We called the cops and when they came the two glasses were still there on the bar, untouched. The cops went to pick up the glasses but Frank said not to touch them. He took a pencil, put it inside the glasses, and lifted them up, preserving a perfect set of prints. Frank knew his stuff. He had been a detective on the French Connection case. The cops eventually picked up the little one in a cop's hangout bar out in Queens, in Astoria. He goes in there, but being short, he's got to hoist himself to get up on the bar stool. As he does, his gun falls through his pant leg and one of the cops picks it up and goes, 'Bang, Bang!'

"I had to go downtown to pick him out of a lineup. I'm in back of a glass window. They said, 'Nobody speak to anybody.' So I looked, and while I was picking him out I turned to the lawyers and said, 'It's number three, but he didn't have earrings on.' But I knew. He colored his hair, and he was wearing earrings. When I was walking out, I saw Frank going in and I showed him three fingers. I said, 'Let's not waste time here.' There was a trial and he was sent up for murder."

Although Elaine has mellowed somewhat over the years, she recently demonstrated that she still packs a wallop when provoked. "It was on a very busy Friday night," Tommy recalls, "and I remember serving this guy who's at the end of the bar a Tanqueray and tonic. He has a girlfriend standing next to him and they are sharing this gin-tonic, passing it back and forth. At the time we had a regular piano player, but he was off that night, and a sub had come in to take his place, a guy who regularly played at a place called Mimi's. The gin-tonic couple were regulars at Mimi's, but they had come to Elaine's to listen to him. They'd never been to Elaine's before. They are standing opposite table four where Elaine is sitting and she takes note of these two exchanging sips of their one drink. 'Hey, you,' she says, 'you going to buy your girlfriend a drink of her own?' This is typical Elaine when she gets going. There's no free lunch. You occupy the real estate, you pay. The guy tosses some inappropriate lingo at her and she says something like, This is no place for a guy who's cheap with his lady friend, whereupon he, who apparently had no idea who she was, got his whole thing going with her, so she finally tells him who he's talking to, but all that does is fire him up and he gets right in her face with, 'Fuck you, lady,' and with that, Elaine whacks him on the jaw and the ring on her hand cuts his cheek, blood running.

"Next thing happens, the guy has dialed the cops and within minutes squad cars are screeching up, a captain, half a dozen cops. The cops come in and march her ouside in handcuffs, but she has to wait at the curb until a female cop arrives to pat her down in case she's got a gun or a bazooka or whatever stashed on her. I go out and tell her to say that this guy stomped her foot and that her natural reaction was to hit him. The cop guarding her says to me, 'Get away from my prisoner, you.' I say, You've got to be kidding me. He says, 'I told you, get away from my prisoner.' I tell him to go screw himself. He says, 'You keep it up and you're going down with her.' I tell Elaine, 'Remember, he stood on your toes,' then I go back inside to see if anyone having dinner is a lawyer.

"Finally, the female cop arrives and frisks Elaine, who is put in a squad car and taken to the lockup where they hold her overnight until bail is set.

"Now this is when it becomes pretty dicey, because if Elaine is found guilty of assault, they could revoke her liquor license, which, for a place like hers, is tantamount to a death sentence. But all her writers rally round and write to the court on her behalf, like James Brady in this colum of his, all of which helped to get the charge dismissed."

STORM THE HOOSEGOW!
ELAINE'S BEEN ARRESTED OVER A BAR ROW
BY JAMES BRADY

New York cops arrested Elaine Kaufman and hauled her off to jail in handcuffs. She was arrested inside her own joint, cuffed and kept at the tenth precinct on assault charges, before being released in the predawn hours of a New York Saturday.

She beat me up, complained a bar customer, male, aged forty-five. Elaine, it was alleged, called him "white trash." She said he got in her face and stepped on her foot.

The plaintiff, said barmen, didn't drink enough (one gin-and-tonic between two of them, with a buck tip). In Manhattan watering places such behavior is considered grounds for surly discontent on the part of the proprietor. If not for actual arrest (of the customer!).

The customer, Tim Sorrels, ended up with a couple of scratches on his right cheek. Which he blames on Elaine. A careful sort, Mr. Sorrels dialed 911 and had an ambulance called. He went to the hospital for treatment that reportedly included anti-snake venom, rabies injection, lockjaw medicine, blood transfusions, biopsies, and a tetanus shot. At press time he was talking of plastic surgeons. And consulting with emi-

The cops come in and march her ouside in handcuffs, but she has to wait at the curb until a female cop arrives to pat her down in case she's got a gun.

nent legal counsel including, say sources, Ginsburg the lawyer.

Mr. Sorrels is from Dallas. Or Arkansas. Accounts vary. Which may explain why he went to Metropolitan Hospital, famed largely as the place where they filmed that George C. Scott black farce, *The Hospital*.

For about thirty-five years Elaine has been running Elaine's, perched on a high stool at the end of the bar, greeting guests, chewing out waiters, and scrutinizing the bills.

Ed Koch goes there. So too John Lindsay. Many Kennedys. Jimmy Carter. Jackie O. Michael Caine. Rockefellers. Sharon Stone. Peter Maas. David Halberstam. Kurt Vonnegut. Gay Talese. Hemingway's pal Hotchner. Paul Newman and Joanne. Streisand. Adventurers and con men. Valentino the fashion designer. Calvin Klein. One night the entire twenty-five Atlanta Braves, with Tom Glavine at our table. Patrick Ewing. Boxers. Treasury agents. Beautiful women. And, a regular with his own table, Woody Allen.

The evening twenty years ago when Rupert Murdoch bought the *New York Post*, in the company of Tip O'Neill and Hugh Carey, arriving at Elaine's at closing time. Even the chef had gone home. Elaine went into the kitchen, hustled up the ham and eggs and toast, and pots of coffee herself, and sat down with Rupert and all of us while we read and reread the front-page story in the *New York Times* about Murdoch's coup.

And it was also at Elaine's during a blizzard that columnist Steve Dunleavy, fatigued from his labors, reclined briefly with a lady in the drifts outside, where a garbage truck ran over his foot. Occasioning, from Pete Hamill, the remark, "I hope it was his writing foot."

Does Mr. Sorrels realize this isn't just a gin mill? This joint is history!

PHOTOGRAPH BY JESSICA BURSTEIN

Tabloid journalism
star Steve Dunleavy

O ne summer night, a volatile argument broke out between the music guru Phil Spector and the *New York Post* columnist Steve Dunleavy at Elaine's. To bolster his invective, Spector whipped out a pistol, a twin of pearl-handled shooters he carries, and pointed it at Dunleavy. Both men had been imbibing rather freely, which probably accounts for the fact that Dunleavy utterly disregarded the gun and punched Spector smartly on the nose causing it to bleed profusely. The following day, in the *New York Post*, Dunleavy wrote a column lauding his performance, under the banner headline: I PUNCHED THE LOUT ON THE SNOUT.

"It was late in the summer, and I was hot—not because of the weather but because I hadn't made Phil Spector's head a bowling ball.

"August 26, 1993, and I'm at Elaine's with a jolly crew, and Spector, with his bizarre hairpiece, walks in. I wouldn't have known him from Herbie Schlotz, who plays the banjo in Brooklyn.

Actor Dominic
Chianese
performs for
the crowd

"But young Shannah Goldner, who was working with all of us at *A Current Affair*, did. She had known him since childhood because her late father, George, was big in the music business.

"To make a long story short—which might be too late—I went to see Shannah, who had joined Phil's table.

"This was because I knew she had been paid, and I was broke. She was a young kid, but I am an equal-opportunity borrower.

"'F— off!' Phil said, without knowing my whispering mission. I left but remembered I had not completed my extortion.

"I returned. Phil had gone to the john. When he returned, he charged at me. 'I've got a gun and I do karate, and I will kick your ass.'

"Deputy Police Commissioner Jack Maple was there, and he stood between us. I got a little testy with that beautiful guy, Jack, because he was preventing me from avenging lost respect.

"Okay, I threw a light punch over Jack's shoulder and hit Phil the dill on the nose. To read about it the next day, you would have thought I took a chainsaw to him.

"That night, Shannah got calls that she recorded on her answering machine from a guy with a Darth Vader voice.

"'We've got your f—ing number. You're dead f—ing meat. I'll break your f—ing legs, your fingers, and your f—ing mother's legs. And tell that gray-haired f— he's dead.'

"I guess he was speaking about *moi.*

"When Shannah called me the next day, I was a little disinterested, since I was doing a story on the Roy DeMeo mob, which had killed seventy-eight guys. I told Shannah if the press asks her, just play them the tape. I was busy with some really bad guys, not a wannabe punk.

"That same day, Nancy Barry, who had known Spector for forty years, got calls. Threats, obscenities, the old routine.

"'Ninety percent of the time Phil was charming, incredibly generous. But that other ten percent, you just ran under a table and waited for the storm to pass,' Nancy told me from Los Angeles.

"'His bad-boy macho was real bad. He was a diabetic who wouldn't take his medication, and a few drinks would make him go nuts. Yes, he was always flashing around guns and wanted to be a macho guy.

"'In those moods, he would love to humiliate people. But not kill.'

"I have two problems. One, he should have been put in an asylum many years ago, despite his genius. And two, I wish I had actually made his head a bowling ball."

Elaine herself has sometimes contributed to nights of physical demonstrations. For instance, the time she threw two garbage can

Ninety percent of the time Phil was charming, incredibly generous. But that other ten percent, you just ran under a table and waited for the storm to pass.

PHOTOGRAPHS BY RON GALELLA

Elaine tries to bean Ron Galella with a garbage can lid

lids at offending paparazzi. "We were being plagued by pesky photographers," barman Tommy says, "especially that nuisance, Ron Galella. It was a Friday, Studio Fifty-four days, Woody Allen was in the restaurant with Mia Farrow at the time. He had just made *Manhattan*. Farrah Fawcett was coming in with her new beau, Ryan O'Neal. That was a big deal at the time. We had photographers up the gazoo. Elaine went out to chase them away from where they were crowding the entrance, and I went with her, both of us taking off down Second Avenue after these turkeys. We are gaining on Ron Galella, who is loaded down with his photo paraphernalia, so Elaine snatches the lid off a garbage container and flings it at him. Turns out it's two lids tied together and as they float through the air, Ron turns around and gets this great shot of Elaine making her pitch. Of course he sells the photo to a gazillion papers and magazines so he gets the last laugh on us."

I n his thirty-three years serving the clientele, Carlo has some astute observations about their eating habits. "From waiting on hundreds of English actors," he says, "actors like Laurence Olivier, Michael Caine, Tom Jones, Albert Finney, Sean Connery, Peter O'Toole, Elizabeth Taylor, I know they prefer broiled fish and chicken, no sauces or spicy food, and they drink scotch and white wine. Now with dancers, like Baryshnikov and Nureyev, they eat steaks black and blue—raw inside, burnt outside—and when I ask them about that, they say it helps dancers build muscle. All the baseball players who come here, Goose Gossage, Bobby Murcer, Jeter, Clemens, Mattingly, Pinella, so many of them, they go for veal chops, osso buco, dishes like that, with martinis and beer, not so much wine. Writers go for oysters, salads, fish, and veal, with martinis and wine—writers like Hamill, Mailer, Plimpton, Talese, Arthur Miller, Nora Ephron. Lots of hockey players in here—Gretsky, Rod Gilbert, Mark Messier, Phil Esposito—they're mostly pasta and beer. Like the long-distance runners who come in, the hockey players say they need endurance for their legs that the pasta gives them. For the Russians who come in, like the four Russian generals during the Gorbachev era, four burly, stocky guys, it's heavy on the vodka and double steaks. Basketball players over the years, like Walt Frazier, Bill Russell, Sam Jones, and Patrick Ewing, it's pasta and steak, wine and beer. Hollywood actresses go for two appetizers, spritzers and Perrier, whereas Broadway actresses prefer pasta and fish with their white wine. Actors like Clint Eastwood, De Niro, Pacino, Peter Falk, Brian Dennehy, and Jack Nicholson are all over the menu and there's no telling what they'll order from the bar."

Hollywood actresses go for two appetizers, spritzers and Perrier, whereas Broadway actresses prefer pasta and fish with their white wine.

"If you ask me, Who is Elaine Kaufman? I'd say she's the Big Mama of them all. The Big Mama and the Big Mother. That's it, in terms of what I do. In a sense, I'm somebody still in the womb, a mother and a motherfucker, but as soon as I come out of my own womb, my own sac, I'll find out who I am, and what I want. You may say, Isn't this rather late in the game for this kind of thing? Well, that's how it is and that's who I am, and while I'm waiting to find out how it all turns out, I'll be having a good time."

—ELAINE

Everyone Comes to Elaine's **16**

Actor Danny Aiello

PHOTOGRAPH BY JESSICA BURSTEIN

*D*iane Becker has been with Elaine for fifteen years and in her role as the restaurant's general manager she is probably closer to Elaine than anyone else. She is as close to her as a daughter, attending to the day-to-day business of the restaurant but also participating in Elaine's personal life, with affection and concern for her well-being. "Elaine has a perpetual fear," Diane says, "that some evening she will open the door and nobody will come. She takes nothing for granted. Every day is like the first day she opened. She has established a high standard for herself and she will never lower the bar."

No night at Elaine's is like any other night. An Englishman comes in with his pet tiger that he puts beside his chair while he eats dinner. Elaine finally ejects both of them when the tiger starts to claw at the waiters. The great French comic Jacques Tati, discusses film financing with Woody.

Danny Zarem with Diane Becker

PHOTOGRAPH BY JESSICA BURSTEIN

The actor John Henry Kurtz tells a date, "I knew you had a lot of luggage from your last relationship, but do I look like an emotional skycap?" Charles Kipps tells a cop's confidential informer who'd fingered a dozen killers, "Lower your voice, not because some mug might want to take revenge, but because you're surrounded by writers and they'll steal your material." The author Jim Harrison eats a whole roast chicken. The literary agent Bob Dattila, explains how his shrink session followed the writer Bob Ward's, and how, twice a week, he'd sit in the waiting room listening to the shrink roaring with laughter as Ward turned his fifty-minute hour into a perfect stand-up routine.

"I met Oscar winner Rita Moreno," Tom Fontana says, "at a party that producer-writer David Black was throwing at Elaine's for the cast of *The Cosby Mysteries* after the show got canceled. Because of that night, I hired her for *Oz*. I met Hell's Angel's president Chuck Zito at Elaine's too. And he became an *Oz* staple."

"I was on my way into Elaine's," David Black says, "when I heard a hooker standing outside telling a cop, 'So the guy says, "Can you do a somersault?" And I say "A somersault?" And the guy says, "You know, you put your head between your legs . . . " And I say, "Honey, if I could put my head between my legs, I wouldn't have been married three times."'"

Chick Vennera, who was in *The Milagro Beanfield War*, tells his table about the army band he'd played in, about how over the years he'd tracked down every musician except one, and, as he is speaking, he looks down the length of Elaine's where Loren, the hired hand, is playing the piano at the bar and exclaims, "That's him! That's him!" Loren was the last band member.

The piano itself is another story. Elaine says, "One day I was

Lower your voice, not because some mug might want to take revenge, but because you're surrounded by writers and they'll steal your material.

having lunch with Sue Barton of Columbia Pictures—we go to the Russian Tea Room—and afterward I say let's go over to Schirmer's piano place, I've been thinking of buying a secondhand piano for when people book a party and they want someone to play or whatever. So we go to Schirmer's and I say to the receptionist, I'm interested in getting a secondhand piano. She pulls out a form and says, What's your name? I give it to her. Your address? Your telephone number? Your occupation? Are you married? Do you play the piano? On and on and on with this questionnaire, when finally I say, Look, I just want to buy a piano, I'm not looking to get fucked. I hauled Sue out of there, the hell with it."

"The next day," the director Sydney Pollack says, "Sue is having lunch with me—I was in New York making *Tootsie* with Dustin—well, Sue tells me about their visit to Schirmer's and it breaks me up. So after lunch, I say, C'mon, Sue, let's go buy the kid a piano. So—complete surprise—on Valentine's Day I send her this piano with a big red ribbon wrapped around it, and I enclosed the questionnaire, which I had filled out."

"I had a piano player here at the bar for a while," Elaine says, "but he played too loud and he sang off-key so I let him go. Nobody really noticed except this one group of people who came in and asked, Where's the piano player? And I said, He's not here anymore. And they said, Oh, we came just for the piano player. I said, When was the last time you were in here? They said, Two years ago. I said, He got tired of waiting. But the piano gets a lot of use—we have loads of weddings here—people who originally met here—and birthdays, book launchings, movie openings, and wakes for the September 11 people, the ones who used to come here. Bob Fosse left some money in his will for his friends to come in and have a good time on him. In the back there—it was a hell of a party. You know, Fosse's still around. You see *Chicago*? He'll always be around."

E laine loves to travel but she's never away for more than a couple of days. "One time she went for two days," Tommy says, "but right away she's on the phone saying, 'I'm coming home.'

"'What do you mean you're coming home? You just got there.'

"'Well, there's nothing happening.'

"'So go out and buy some wine, do something, hire a car, go somewhere. Everything's fine here.' All of us who work for her love Elaine. I love the bones of Elaine, as a person and as a woman. She has been very, very good to me. She cares about me. My wife thinks she's the greatest thing since sliced bread."

There were a couple of summers when Elaine did manage to stay away from the restaurant, the summers she rented a yacht in the Mediterranean so she could swim in the Bosphorus. Her unrealized wish, however, is to own a Learjet so she could occasionally fly to Europe for a weekend. Over the years her savvy clients have advised her on the stock market with bountiful results but Elaine spends very conservatively; and although the jet is affordable, she will resolutely keep it on her wish list. But the often repeated item that she is taking flying lessons is simply Elaine in the throes of a particularly boring interview, making up a whopper to enliven the process. Once it appeared in print, it was picked up in subsequent publications as gospel. Elaine guffaws over this. "I can't even drive a car," she says.

"It's amazing, the success of this place," Tommy says. "We don't do any local business at all. Nobody walks into this place. Everybody comes by car, taxi, limousine, or what have you. And some people come on a bike, like George Plimpton. We never advertise. The clientele here is absolutely mind-boggling. It's her personality. It's her dedication to detail. 'Don't tell me about what they're doing across the street, I want to attend to that party of four that's here.' That's her personality. And Elaine's big thing, always quoted, is 'Don't tell me what we did yesterday. Don't tell me what we're going to do tomorrow. What are we doing today? Now, right now.'"

You ask me— forty years— Elaine, What was the highlight? That was. The night Jackie came in to dance.

Asked to name one moment during the cavalcade of forty years that she cherishes above all others, Elaine unhesitatingly says, "The time that Jackie Kennedy came, two o'clock one morning. Unannounced, unexpected, there's a commotion at the door, a lively group is on the way in, led by Mike Nichols and Susan Sontag, followed by Adolph Greene and Betty Comden and George Plimpton, and last in, Leonard Bernstein, who is escorting Jackie Kennedy. It was her first night out after her mourning period and the group was trying to cheer her up. They started up the jukebox, popped Champagne, and I went into the kitchen and made a big antipasto. Everyone started to dance to the music, Lennie was dancing with Jackie, who was very beautiful. She was wearing a Chanel gold bouclé suit with a starburst emerald brooch. Betty and Adolph started to sing with the music, and at one point Lennie sat down and did his thing at the piano. It was an unforgettable night.

"I couldn't take my eyes off Jackie, the way she moved, as we all waltzed around the bar, the sweetness of her smile, how delicate

PHOTOGRAPH BY JESSICA BURSTEIN

she was—an honest-to-God superstar. She was trying to get into the spirit of things but I could tell not all of her was there that night. The way she lost that man. She was First Lady, all right—you don't get more first than she was. She came in many times after that. Sat in the back there. I started to put her with her back to the door—for privacy—but she preferred facing forward: She had a smile for everyone. You ask me—forty years—Elaine, What was the highlight? That was. The night Jackie came in to dance."

At one time, a piano player briefly held forth at the bar but he interfered with the ebb and flow that is peculiarly Elaine's, so both player and piano were soon banished

Elaine is, in essence, a fictional character, compounded of one part Damon Runyon's Nicely Nicely Johnson and one part Dorothy Parker's "Big Blonde." She has the dramatic presence of Sophie Tucker, the brassiness of Rosie O'Donnell, and the street smarts of Toots Shor. As a matter of fact, one night, around two in the morning, Elaine, Bobby Short, and a few others were at PJ Clarke's, having a drink with Danny Lavezzo, when a waiter came over and informed Elaine that Toots, who was also there, wanted to meet her. A few moments later, the hulking figure of Toots appeared at Elaine's table, a bit unsteady from a long stint of drinking. He studied her for a while, then he said, "Elaine, I just wanted to take a look at my successor," whereupon he departed.

Elaine is indeed the successor of all the big-timers who went before her. She presides over her uptown domain with benignity, unpredictable wit, two-fisted pugnaciousness, and a remarkable insight into the human condition. Behind her large eyeglasses, her eyes miss nothing that transpires, eyes of laughter, of compassion, of fury. She is just as insecure about her success as she was the first day she opened, knowing full well the fickleness of the restaurant-going, nightlife saloon public, so she works assiduously at maintaining the curious ambience that is her place's hallmark. "I live a party life," she says. "Elsa Maxwell used to have to send out invitations. I just open the door."

The poet Fred Seidel, one of her first customers, has written this valedictory in his poem "Pressed Duck":

Elaine said, "Why do we
Need anybody
Else? We're the world."

ENDNOTE

As this book was going to press, we received word of the death of George Plimpton, whose witty reminiscences about Elaine's illuminate many of these pages. I first met George in Madrid in 1954 when he came to interview Hemingway for *The Paris Review*, and we remained good and fast friends over the years. Many's the time we swapped stories at Elaine's writers' table, often joined by Elaine herself who, quite simply, adored George, one of her "founding" writers. There is a plaster bust of George prominently situated on a shelf in the center of the restaurant and Elaine intends to keep it there forever.

—A.E.H

INDEX

Page numbers in italics refer to illustrations.

PHOTOGRAPH CREDITS

Many of the photographs in this book were taken by the noted photographer Jessica Burstein, who, for the past decade, at Elaine's request, has made the restaurant an unobtrusive studio where she focuses on the array of notables who enter the preserve. Jessica's photographs have appeared in many major publications. She is the official photographer for the *Law & Order* television series. Her most recent books are *The Grandmother Book* (St. Martin's Press, 2000) and *Law & Order Crime Scenes* (Barnes & Noble, 2003).

Jessica Burstein: vi, xiv, xx, 12, 15, 19, 28, 45, 50, 64, 76, 79, 83, 86, 88, 91, 98, 113, 115, 123, 127, 157, 163, 169, 172, 177, 181, 186, 203, 207, 213, 214, 218, 220, 225.

Elaine Kaufman Collection: 3, 25, 32, 37, 53, 61, 67, 71, 105, 118, 121, 134, 136, 140, 148, 149, 151, 152, 192, 195.

Jonathan Becker: 101, 154, 174, 197, 204.

Ron Galella: 40, 108, 216.

Sally Davies: 76. Special thanks also to Sally for her digital photography work throughout.

Walter Bernard: 134.

Nora Ephron and Nicholas Pileggi Collection: 102.